ILLUSTRATED HISTORY OF THE VIE...

KU-350-311

BANTAM BOOKS

TORONTO ● NEW YORK ● LONDON ● SYDNEY ● AUCKLAND

SKY SOLDIERS

by

F. Clifton Berry, Jr.

CLEARING THE IRON TRIANGLE

With its network of secret tunnels, the Viet Cong stronghold less than an hour from Saigon was a constant threat to the security of the capital.

Twice the Sky Soldiers cleared it, but each time the enemy returned.

DAK TO & HILL 875

Flamethrower at the ready, paratroopers advance on an enemy position. Hill 875 was the most fortified NVA position the Sky Soldiers encountered.

DAK TO & HILL 875
Dug into their foxholes,
M-16s at the ready,
troopers wait for the next
attack. The action lasted
six days before the enemy
was driven from the hill.

EDITORS: Richard Grant, Richard Ballantine. PHOTO RESEARCH: John Moore.
DRAWINGS: John Batchelor. MAPS: Peter Williams. STUDIO: Kim Williams.
PRODUCED BY: The Up & Coming Publishing Company, Bearsville, New York.

SKY SOLDIERS:
THE ILLUSTRATED HISTORY OF THE VIETNAM WAR
A Bantam Book/ August 1987

AUTHOR'S NOTE

*Unit designations throughout the book follow US military practice with the
smallest unit cited first. Thus 1st Squad, 2d Platoon, Company A, 3d
Battalion, 503d Infantry Regiment. "Regiment" is omitted in US military
usage. Second and later mentions of a battalion are usually shortened to 2d
Bn, 503; or 2/503. Times are given by the 24-hour clock. Thus 0035 is 35
minutes after midnight; 1400 is 2:00 p.m.*

ACKNOWLEDGEMENTS

*The author wishes to thank former commanders of the 173d Airborne
Brigade (Separate) for their help: They all were gracious and helpful with
recollections, documents, and referrals to other persons. Officers and men of
the brigade also helped with recreating the past. Experts at the Army's
Center for Military History responded with insights, documents, and
directions. Special thanks are due to Dr. John Schlight, George MacGarrigle,
Mrs. M. Sawyer, and John Wilson. Finally, the staff at the Army Adjutant
General's Office and the Federal Archives and Record Center were unsparing
in their help with threading the way through the boxes of thousands of
documents about the 173d and its units. To those persons and the others
who have helped with this project, I shall always be grateful. They are free
from responsibility for errors. I bear the burden of those.*

*Photographs for this book were selected from the archives of DAVA and
Military Archive Research Services*

Library of Congress Cataloging-in-Publication Data
Berry, F. Clifton, Jr.
Sky Soldiers

1. Vietnamese Conflict, 1961-1975—Regimental histories—United States. 2.
United States. Army. Airborne Brigade, 173rd—History. I.Title.
DS558.4.B47 1987   959.704'34   86-47565
ISBN 0-553-34320-3

Published simultaneously in the United States and Canada

PRINTED IN THE UNITED STATES OF AMERICA

CW   0   9   8   7   6   5   4   3   2

Contents

Welcome and Deploy

Quick-reaction operations

THE FIRST men of the 173d Airborne Brigade to arrive in Vietnam slept for most of the six-hour flight from Okinawa.

They landed at Bien Hoa, outside Saigon, at sunrise on May 5, 1965. As the rear cargo ramps were lowered on the C-130 transport planes they felt a blast of heat and humidity, even at 0530 hours. It was an uncomfortable welcome to a war.

The 173d Airborne Brigade (Separate), to give the unit its full title, was created in 1963 to be the US Army's elite troubleshooting reserve in the Pacific theatre. It was the Army's first ground combat unit committed to Vietnam, and one of the last to leave. Its troopers were all volunteers for airborne duty, and that unique bond was to help them to write a short but glorious chapter in US military annals. The brigade was some 5,000 men strong at any one time, but more than 35,000 served with it during six years of combat in Vietnam. They were nicknamed 'Sky Soldiers' and 1,533 made the ultimate sacrifice for their country.

An American adviser who had been out in the field with an ARVN battalion watched the paratroopers unload. In his tour, he had become accustomed to the small-framed Vietnamese and the austerity of their equipment. He was astonished at the size of the brawny paratroopers, and the extent of the gear they unloaded. To him, the arrival of the 173d at Bien Hoa signaled a welcome change in the war. He no longer felt alone.

The troopers themselves were surprised at the size of the installations they had been assigned to protect at Bien Hoa and Vung Tau, east of Saigon. In the shimmering light of the tropic day the bases seemed to stretch to the horizon. Guard towers

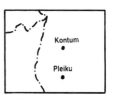

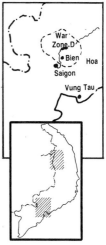

Welcome and Deploy

WELCOME TO THE WAR: The date is May 5, 1965 — Day One of the 173d's deployment. Within hours of disembarking from their C-130 transports the Sky Troopers found themselves guarding the perimeter of the airbase where they had landed. Within days the brigade spread out, assigned to defend the vital complex of bases around Saigon. But few thought that this elite force would remain on sentry duty for long.

poked up at intervals around the perimeter. Sandbag and metal revetments protected the parked aircraft. Air policemen passed in their patrolling jeeps, three men and a swivelling .30 caliber machine gun protecting the base from inside the miles of wire on its perimeter.

The constant noise of air operations also pounded on the senses. When the paratroopers surveyed the ramp at the Bien Hoa base they saw and heard aircraft moving in every direction. A-1E Skyraiders with their big four-bladed propellers rumbled and roared; the turboprop engines of C-130 Hercules transports keened shrilly while their props emitted a throaty low frequency that rattled their skulls. And the pure jet blast of fighters like the F-100 Super Sabre split the air. Underlying all those noises was the stead 'wop-wop-wop' of the rotors of hundreds of helicopters coming and going, night and day.

Insignia of the 173d — The first Army combat unit into Vietnam, the 173d had been formed only two years earlier. But it could trace its lineage as the Army's only separate airborne brigade back to the 503d Parachute Battalion of World War II.

While the units were arriving and settling in, the brigade's infantry, the first and second battalions of the 503d Regiment, began the transition to combat. They accompanied ARVN units in sending out ambush patrols at night. Within three days, they were mounting their own ambushes. Three days after arrival, three officers and three noncommissioned officers from 2/503 went on an airmobile operation with the ARVN 48th Regiment. On May 10, one of the NCOs, Staff Sergeant Boyd, was wounded while on the ARVN operation. He became the first 173d trooper to receive a combat wound.

As the infantry battalions moved into combat by active patrolling in the two base areas, the other elements of the brigade were still arriving in Vietnam. The 3d Battalion, 319th Field Artillery came by sea, arriving on May 12. It established firing positions for its 105mm howitzers to support the infantry and patrols. On Sunday, May 16, the 173d's commander, General Butch Williamson pulled the lanyard to fire the 319's first artillery combat round. That night, the 3/319 began firing harassing and interdictory (H&I) fire against suspected enemy positions and trail routes. H&I fire were always controversial. Advocates claimed the firing kept the enemy off balance and unsure whether he had been located. Critics bitched that it wasted ammunition and kept friendly troops awake. The Viet Cong

The remote jungle island of Iriomote in the Ryukyus chain —a year before their arrival in Vietnam the 173d used it as a training ground. Their commander warned that Iriomote would "tax physical endurance and mental toughness to the utmost."

troops in the immediate areas of 173d units were slow to react against their presence. However, the Hanoi state radio took notice: 'Hanoi Hannah,' one of the English-language broadcasters, reported the 173d's arrival, calling them "Juvenile delinquents in green undershirts."

With all of its elements in position, the brigade began extending the reach of its combat power. By May 10, General Williamson was reporting to the High Command that the 173d had begun its airmobile training with UH-1D 'Huey' helicopters. And all the time the brigade was honing its jungle-warfare skills.

The tiniest detail could not be overlooked in jungle fighting. Forgetting insect repellent at night, for instance, could mean torture from the flying bugs that filled the air close to the ground. But on an ambush, or moving through enemy territory, the troops did not use insect repellent. They had learned to prefer the torments of insects, because the repellent's unique smell could give away their location. When moving in enemy territory, walking the point was the riskiest place. The point man was the first man, out ahead of everyone else. His job was to see the enemy first, or be seen and shot at by the enemy. In either case, his role was to alert his buddies behind. Obviously this was a very risky job. So within the point squad of a platoon, the job of point man would rotate. And within the point platoon of a company, the job of point squad would be rotated.

Some men had special talents for walking the point. They were adept at spotting the clues of ambush or enemy presence fast. People in their squads felt safer when they were on the point. Others were not as talented, and endangered those behind them.

The month of May saw squads, platoons, and companies moving further and further out into the jungle. Meanwhile, the battalion and brigade staffs concentrated on polishing their procedures for coordinating and controlling their own and supporting units.

The object was to ensure that the commanders and staffs could 'orchestrate' a battle when it came. To the troops engaging the enemy, a firefight was kill or be killed and support your buddies. Your instinct for survival and your training kept you functioning. You loaded and fired your weapon and threw grenades as if there were no tomorrow. If you didn't, there might not be.

To the senior officers, not in the midst of the blood and noise of battle, the fight was different. A battle meant bringing in supporting fire and whatever was needed to win the fight.

Inexperienced unit commanders have a tendency to throw in supporting fire in sequence. That is, they will call for mortar and artillery fire. When it is done, they might call in an air strike. That finished, they will bring in resupply of ammunition or reinforcing troops in helicopters. Then they might resume the artillery.

This tendency must be overcome. Artillery, close air support, and reinforcing helicopter lift should be planned and executed so that one does not have to wait on the other. It is hard for some people to visualize these things all at the same time: the landscape of the battlefield, the artillery trajectories, the flight paths of the attack aircraft, and the routes of the helicopters snaking along near to the treetops. But a commander who wants to preserve the lives of his men up front will train his mind to do just that. He keeps the artillery and air crashing in on the enemy while the reinforcing helicopters approach

IN COMMAND:
Brig. Gen. Ellis 'Butch' Williamson, the 173d's first commander in Vietnam, directing a Ranger patrol officer during operations at Bien Hoa. The white star atop the parachute wings above his left pocket denotes a Senior Parachutist, with more than 30 jumps.

and land. Then he shifts fire so the reinforcements can shoot their own weapons and maneuver to engage the enemy. The process takes time and practice to develop. It also requires a high level of confidence and trust between the participating infantry and supporting arms.

At the end of May, the brigade conducted a four-day operation that included airmobile assaults on three different objectives and the security of a fourth. This first operation met relatively light

Welcome and Deploy

EARLY DAYS:
Publicity shot of a perimeter guard taken on the day the 173d landed. The M-16 rifle and the M79 grenade launcher were basic infantry weapons in Vietnam. The M-16 is steadied on a folding bipod for accuracy when fired on automatic. Note the Sky Trooper's clean-cut appearance and the relative lack of spare ammunition. When the action became real, holes were dug deeper and ammunition was carried by the boxload.

opposition, but it contributed to the stock of combat lessons learned. In addition, by using support troops in combat roles, it reinforced the close confidence and mutual respect among men of the units. While the other units were in the operation area 17 kilometers away, the Support Battalion formed a task force to continue the security mission at Bien Hoa. There were no 'rear' and 'front line' distinctions.

These operations were clearly beyond the brigade's

immediate assignment on the security perimeters of Bien Hoa and Vung Tau. Back in Washington questions were raised whether the mission of American forces had changed from defensive to offensive. General Westmoreland was not about to change his policy. He quoted Secretary of State Dean Rusk, who admitted on television that "we don't expect these men to sit there like hypnotized rabbits waiting for the Viet Cong to strike."

To the troopers and commanders of the 173d

Brigade, operations beyond the perimeter contributed directly to the security mission. On June 10, the 1st Battalion, Royal Australian Regiment (1/RAR) arrived in Vietnam to fight with the 173d.

Its ranks included many veterans of jungle combat in Malaysia. In addition to the infantry battalion, the force included a troop of armored personnel carriers, an engineer company, a signal company, and a helicopter detachment. It was a well balanced force, except for artillery. In due course a

WALKING POINT:
In enemy territory the point man was first man out. Because of the danger, the job of walking point rotated within a squad.

New Zealand artillery battery with lightweight 105 mm guns arrived, and was given priority to supporting the Australians.

The 1/RAR was ready for combat almost immediately after arrival. In fact, less than three

weeks after it arrived, the 173d included 1/RAR with
its own infantry battalions in the largest helicopter
troop lift yet in Vietnam. It was a foray into War
Zone D, and was the first time in more than a year
that large friendly units had penetrated that VC

TIME OUT:
Under fire, a
machine gunner
drops hastily to
the ground.

The RTO — surrounded by jungle a radiotelephone operator was a unit's link with the outside world beyond the immediate field of vision. Through the RTO a unit commander could control fire support, call for medical evacuation and coordinate maneuvers with neighboring units.

stronghold. Friendly forces also included two battalions of the Vietnamese 2d Airborne Brigade, and the 48th ARVN Regiment. Additional fire support came from E Troop, 17th Cavalry and Company D, 16th Armor, the brigade's armored elements.

The helicopter lift used more than 144 Army aircraft, and made more than ten sorties each from 77 troop carrier helicopters.

The Australians were used in quick reaction operations, followed by aggressive patrolling as all units experienced steady contact with VC forces. This operation foreshadowed the later pattern. The allied troops moved into an area, made contact with the VC, engaged in fire-fights to press the assault. The VC withdrew, the allied troops followed up and found caches of rice, weapons, and equipment. The caches were boobytrapped. While the caches were searched and casualties treated, the VC waited. The allies dug in and built defensive perimeters. Eventually, usually after nightfall, VC small arms and mortar fire would hit the defensive position. The allies responded with flares over the battlefield and defensive fire. With daylight, the units would move out again to search the area and make contact again.

On July 6, the brigade moved into War Zone D again, to clear an area just north of the Dong Nai river (Song Dong Nai), immediately south of the preceding operation area.

The 48th ARVN Regiment blocked enemy escape to the west. The Dong Nai River was an obstacle to south and east. To the north the 173d's three battalions, 1/503, 2/503 and 1/RAR, made the airmobile assaults to close the trap, supported by fire from 3/319 Artillery, Company D, 16th Armor, and the 173d Engineer Company from across the river.

First contact with the enemy was light, but built up in volume and intensity as the days passed. By the second day, the infantry battalions were encountering Viet Cong companies in full uniform. The VC were defending a large base area. One complex capable of housing 800 - 1,200 men was found by 1/503. It was complete with mess halls, classrooms, latrines, and extensive tunnel system. The area contained more than 150 booby traps.

When the four-day operation ended, the brigade's haul included a ton of documents, 30 weapons, and 28 POWs. It had damaged the D800 VC battalion, a main force unit. On withdrawal, to give some idea of the complexity of the operation, three thousand troops were lifted out of three different landing zones (LZs) in just three hours, ten minutes.

While they were pulling out of the center LZ, friendly troops were still in the western LZ. Helicopter gunships were hitting a circle around the center LZ, and another helicopter strike was running in a north-south direction. They also had the artillery firing high angle fire to screen the northern side of the LZ. The troop lift helicopters came in under the artillery fire. All this while an air strike was going in to the northeast.

In August 1965, the brigade flew to the Pleiku-Kontum areas in the Central Highlands. Increased enemy pressure against Special Forces camps near the Cambodian border in the highlands, especially against the camp at Duc Co, brought the call. As the VC raised the force against Duc Co to regimental strength, the ARVN reinforced the camp. The relief column became heavily engaged. The ARVN high command needed more reinforcements to permit them to pass their reserves into the fight if necessary, and also to hold key terrain around the Thanh Binh pass so their forces could withdraw. The 173d was given the mission. It committed more than 2500 men to the operation for almost a month.

The Claymore mine was a deadly defensive weapon. It consisted of 700 steel balls embedded in high explosive in a curved casing with fold-out legs. It was designed to produce a killing zone by exploding in a fan-shaped area in front of the mine, leaving a safe area behind it.

The Claymore was planted in the right spot, then wires were led from it and rigged to explode the device in one of two ways. The trooper who emplaced it could 'command detonate' the Claymore himself when an enemy entered the mine's killing zone. That was useful in defensive positions, when the troops waited until the enemy was in the killing zone. The other way to detonate Claymores was by trip wire. The wires would be set up across trails or other likely spots. When an enemy foot pulled on the wire, the Claymores blew up, killing everything in their deadly fan.

The ARVN needed help urgently. In the first week of the operation, from August 10 - 17, the brigade ran

The Claymore —Detonated by remote control, the Claymore mine threw 700 iron pellets in a fan-shaped blast.

Welcome and Deploy

HUEY LANDING: The 173d was unused to heliborne operations when it first landed in Vietnam. The situation soon changed. Here troopers race from an LZ (Landing Zone) three weeks after arrival in Vietnam. As the UH-1D lifts off, door gunners stand ready. Along with point men, door gunners, frequently easy targets, suffered high casualty rates.

43 company-size, 116 platoon-size, and 22 squad-size operations, plus 22 platoon-to-company-size quick reaction 'Eagle Flights.'

After the ARVN relief column withdrew through Thanh Binh, the brigade returned to Pleiku. It spent the next two weeks searching out and destroying enemy forces in the Pleiku-Kontum area.

In its first four months of combat, the 173d Airborne Brigade (Separate) had established itself as

a formidable fighting force. It had airborne mobility and the mental flexibility that went with it. It had penetrated War Zone D three times, flown to operate in the Highlands, and still continued the original security missions around Bien Hoa and Vung Tau. The high command had come to depend on the 173d when it needed something difficult done. It had won a reputation which would be tested many times.

Into the Triangle

Operations Hump and Crimp

THE 173d's combat tempo picked up as the rainy season waned in the autumn of 1965, with another major foray into War Zone D from September 14 to 28. This time the brigade was to find and destroy suspected large enemy units. Intelligence was sketchy, but a regiment, a couple of battalions, and several company-size units were suspected. Their permanent installations were thought to be just outside artillery range of the ARVN position at Ben Cat. More than 190 enemy contacts were made in the two weeks of action.

A major result of the operation was capturing supplies and gaining intelligence information. Company C, 1/503, itself captured 62 Russian sniper rifles with telescopes, 4,500 hand grenades, 91 Bangalore torpedoes (explosive tubes used to blow a path through barbed wire), and 36 military radios.

During the second week of October 1965, the brigade entered and swept the Iron Triangle region 30 kilometers northwest of Saigon, until then considered inviolate enemy territory. More than 20 years of construction had turned it into a maze of tunnels, supply dumps, hospitals, schools, rest areas, and training camps.

Little was really known about the area except that it was covered by very dense jungle, and in General Williamson's words, "the enemy fired at everyone that came close." No friendly forces, not even small intelligence patrols, had been into the area for years.

Thus, the intelligence information given to the 173d was scanty. It warned that the area was heavily mined and booby-trapped. Intelligence reports also estimated that the low, matted and entangled growth made it impractical for the Viet Cong to construct major permanent camps in a large part of the

area. However, large tunnel systems were believed to be in the area, used as aid stations, training camps, unit headquarters, and supply dumps. The reports contradicted themselves, but that was not new, particularly for an area where friendly troops had not actually been on the ground.

The terrain in the Iron Triangle was fairly level, rising a few meters above the rivers. It was covered by patches of dense second-growth jungle mingled with the low, matted undergrowth of bamboo and other foliage.

Into the Triangle

MOVING OUT: Camouflage sweat towels at their necks, Sky Troopers wade through a rice field amid the rotor downwash of a departing UH-1D that had just inserted them into a potential combat zone near Vo Dat northeast of Saigon. In the early days locating the elusive VC was a major problem. So was the heat. To combat dehydration salt tablets were issued. These men are carrying the new model flexible plastic water bottles as well as the old belt-hung canteens.

The 173d's operation began on October 8 and ended on October 14. Its object was to clear the environs of Ben Cat and to open Highway 13 for introduction of 1st Infantry Division units into the area. Without the clearing operation, the enemy forces operating from the sanctuary of the Iron Triangle would be a continuous threat to the 1st Infantry Division, as well as to Saigon.

The brigade was organized into four task forces for the operation. Three were built around the infantry battalions (1/503, 2/503, and 1/RAR) and the

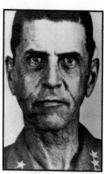

Maj. Gen Jonathan O. Seaman —commander of the 1st Infantry Division. During sweeps into the Iron Triangle he was in operational control of the 173d. Like Brig. Gen. Williamson, he believed the sweeps had cleared the area. But on each occasion the Viet Cong re-emerged from their tunnels.

fourth around the 3/319 Artillery. On D-Day, the four task forces of the brigade moved into position. Heavy artillery preparation, fighter air-strikes, and two massive B-52 strikes hit the area ahead of the movements.

The scheme of maneuver had the task forces sweeping south, then east. On the western flank 1/503 would work down the Saigon river. On its left 2/503 would be plodding through the center of the area. Anchored in turn on its left was TF 1/RAR.

The task forces swept through the 50-square-kilometer area of thick jungle in good order. Ground opposition was light. However, the enemy fired readily at helicopters and airplanes, hitting five C-123s and nine helicopters.

As in the operation weeks before, large numbers of booby traps and command-detonated mines were encountered. And the brigade commander said: "We spent the days fussing and fighting the elements in the form of thick jungle, bomb blast areas, intense heat, and little water."

Because Highway 13, which ran into the Triangle, was not secure, most resupply was by air. There was no airstrip at the forward supply point, so the logistical system depended on helicopters, parachute airdrops of supplies, and low level extractions.

In his report on the operation, General Williamson said: "The Iron Triangle is no more." He also said, "The Iron Triangle that once consisted of fifty square kilometers of the unknown has now been destroyed. . . . The few installations that we could not destroy at the time have now been definitely pinpointed and can be destroyed at will by air attacks. One more enemy bulwark has been completely marked off the situation map."

Based on what he and his men encountered in their six days tromping through the jungle, General Williamson was justified. However, he was wrong.

The 173d had barely scratched the surface. The enemy avoided contact. He chose to evade contact and use mines and booby traps to fight his battle. The 173d and other US units would have to return to the Iron Triangle again and again. Its fortifications were too massive for destruction by a single brigade. In fact, the Iron Triangle was never neutralized.

On November 1, the 173d came under operational

control of 1st Infantry Division, commanded by Major General Jonathan O. Seaman. On the same day, the brigade was entertained at base camp by the Martha Raye show. The searing hot weather at Bien Hoa did not prevent the troops' enjoying the respite from the jungle.

November 5 saw the beginning of the brigade's fifth excursion into War Zone D. The brigade planners named it Operation Hump. By then the term 'hump' was part of the airborne language. It expressed the troopers' feelings about carrying heavy loads through the jungle. Operation Hump resulted in the heaviest fighting in a single day up to that time. It took the brigade back into the part of War Zone D north of the Dong Nai river, about 25 kilometers north of Bien Hoa.

In Hump the brigade used small five-man long-range patrols as well as sweeping with platoon, company, and battalion sized forces. The long-range patrols were lifted into areas not covered by other units, where they watched quietly for enemy forces. When enemy units were spotted, they were able to call in air strikes and artillery, then slip away.

On Operation Hump the enemy chose to stand and fight on several occasions. The Australians captured

INVADING THE TRIANGLE: US strategists described the Viet Cong stronghold 20 miles northwest of Saigon as "like a dagger pointing at the heart of the capital." On October 8, 1965, the Australian Task Force (RAR) moved into the zone from the north while the 173d's two battalions, the 1/503 and 2/503, were heli-lifted into two LZs (landing zones). The three infantry battalions then swept through the Triangle but met little opposition from an enemy going into hiding.

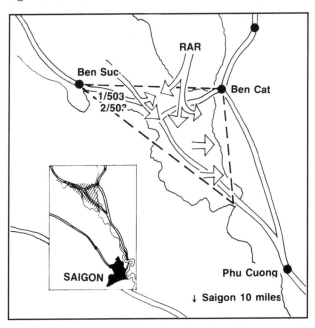

95996 USAF

Into the Triangle

AIR SUPPORT:
A pallet is pushed out from a Hercules C-130 some 300 feet above a helicopter LZ. Para-dropping supplies by this method was soon replaced by the precise delivery method known as LAPES — Low Altitude Parachute Extraction System (inset). Supplies were lashed to pallets on the floor of the cargo bay. Approaching the drop point the crew released the restraints and popped a small chute out the rear door. The chute pulled the load clear, slowing its speed enough to keep it in one piece on landing.

35

a prisoner who carried a plan for an attack by a larger VC force on the Bien Hoa area. With information from him, 1/RAR, using its own observation pilot and patrols, located the larger VC force. By calling in artillery fire and air strikes, and pursuing with a patrol, the Australians forced the VC platoon to move into the arms of an Australian company waiting to capture them.

Hard intelligence information came to the brigade during the day on November 7. It confirmed that a major VC force was situated only two kilometers west of 1/503. The battalion sent out small patrols in that direction just before dark. They soon confirmed the intelligence. The patrols were drawn into the battalion perimeter for the night. As darkness settled, the stage was set for the major confrontation that was to develop the next day on Hill 65.

On the 8th, Company C of 1/503 moved out first toward the enemy with two platoons on line. Company B followed. Company A and the battalion headquarters were kept in reserve. At 0800, Company C's right platoon was hit with heavy small arms and automatic weapons fire. As its other platoons joined the action, it became apparent that Company C's 100-plus paratroopers had locked in with an enemy battalion. These were North Vietnamese Army main force soldiers, wearing uniforms and steel helmets, well armed and with apparently limitless ammunition.

The enemy battalion began to encircle Company C. The commander of 1/503 moved his Company B into the action. It soon became locked in hand-to-hand combat with the enemy. Men fired their rifles, grenade launchers, and machine guns until they overheated. They threw grenades at close range, and hacked at the enemy with machetes and entrenching tools. The enemy, screaming and yelling like the paratroopers, stood and fought the same way. It was hard to see more than 10-20 meters ahead, but that didn't matter, because the enemy was that close. He clung desperately to the rifle companies, hoping to prevent the brigade from using gunships and air strikes on him by staying too close.

Companies B and C fought hard and linked up, but the enemy began to encircle Company B's unprotected right flank. Now Company A, the reserve, was also committed to the fight.

The fighting was so close that supporting fire and air strikes had to be placed behind the enemy. The infantrymen poured small arms, grenades, and machine gun fire on the front of the enemy while the artillery and air chewed at his rear. The enemy force continued to cling to 1/503 as the day passed, making assault after assault. The jungle was so dense and the fighting so close that no resupply or evacuation was possible. The troops stood their ground and fought. Their mouths were dry from yelling, but their bodies were slick and their jungle fatigues black with sweat. In pauses in the fighting, they redistributed ammunition and tended their wounded. General Williamson planned to jump in, but darkness and the height of the trees ruled that out.

By late afternoon, enemy fire slackened to sniper and sporadic machine gun bursts. Light harassing fire continued through the night. At the battalion command post perimeter 1,000 meters to the east of the embattled companies, small groups of enemy soldiers brushed with outposts through the night. The enemy was withdrawing his survivors from the battlefield, but the troops in the perimeter could not know that in the dark jungle. No helicopter could

Staff Sgt. Larry Pierce —mortally wounded when he dived on an enemy anti-personnel mine to protect his men from the blast. He posthumously received the Medal of Honor.

PFC Milton Olive III —awarded the Medal of Honor posthumously for his gallantry in throwing himself on an enemy grenade lobbed into the middle of his squad. He was 18 years old.

land in the deep jungle where Companies B and C fought.

By early morning of the 9th, seven power saws had been lowered to the force to augment the men's own tools. Trees up to 250 feet high and six feet in diameter were cut down, creating a funnel 250 feet deep and about 80 feet in diameter. Williamson's command helicopter was the first to snake its way down the funnel at first light. He stayed on the ground and walked out with the troops when the action was over. For the rest of the day, helicopter

Into the Triangle

IN CONTACT:
Paratroopers firing M-16s engage a Viet Cong position in the jungle northeast of Bien Hoa in February 1966. Capable of emptying one of its 20-round magazines in approximately three seconds, the M-16 could land a useful volume of fire on target—providing it did not jam. After an incident at Khe Sanh when the M-16 was blamed for Marine deaths on the battlefield, the M-16 became the subject of a congressional investigation. Subsequently better powder was introduced and later models upgraded.

pilots managed to maneuver their aircraft down into the funnel, where they evacuated the wounded and dead.

Later on the afternoon of November 9, 1/RAR joined 1/503. They were airlifted out from a slightly larger landing zone in the jungle that could accommodate three ships.

After the battle, the enemy force was identified as the Q-761 Regiment. It is estimated that it was four to five times the strength of the companies of 1/503 that fought it. The Q-761 left 408 bodies on the battlefield. Friendly casualties on November 8 were 50 killed and 82 wounded.

During the action, the Air Force flew 117 fighter-bomber sorties, delivering 158 tons of ordnance, and the artillery fired 5,352 rounds totalling 160 tons.

The brigade continued operations without let-up through November and December. By December 22 the 173d was withdrawn back to its Bien Hoa base, ready to celebrate its first of six Christmases in Vietnam.

Playboy magazine was a hot topic at Christmas time. Hugh Hefner, the publisher, had advertised that anyone who bought a lifetime subscription to the magazine would have the first copy delivered by a *Playboy* Playmate. One of the platoons of Company B, 2d Battalion, 503d Infantry, took up a collection. They bought a lifetime subscription for their platoon leader, Lieutenant Jack Price. Now they

were waiting to learn if the publisher would make good on his promise. . . .

To start the new year of 1966, the 173d launched Operation Marauder on January 1. Its task forces moved before first light by road and air into the Mekong delta and the Plain of Reeds area.

Using the airfield at Bao Trai as the command post and artillery base, the 173d moved its infantry battalions along both banks of the Oriental river, searching for VC units. At the same time, its armor (Company D, 16th Armor and the Australian Prince of Wales Light Horse) and Troop E, 17th Cavalry, searched the areas around Bao Trai. Results of the operation included significant damage to the 267th VC Battalion and overrunning the headquarters of the 506th VC Battalion. In these fights the VC again clung to the US units they were engaging, by contrast with earlier practice of withdrawing upon

Into the Triangle

READY FOR ACTION: Troopers race through the high grass to clear an LZ and get into position for an attack during Operation Marauder near the Oriental river.

Into the Triangle

TUNNEL RATS: Colt .45 automatic at the ready, a Sky Soldier heads underground in search of Viet Cong. The high casualty rate among soldiers sent into tunnels led to the formation of specialist squads known as the tunnel rats. Their equipment was kept to a minimum. In the hot, dark, and cramped underground warrens where ambushes were frequent, a tunnel rat would carry just a flashlight, a handgun, a knife, and a length of rope to retrace his steps or haul out a wounded comrade.

contact. Midway through Operation Marauder Company B, 2/503 Infantry, had a hard firefight. Lieutenant Jack Price, the *Playboy* subscriber, was wounded and evacuated to a field hospital. Now the question was whether the magazine's publisher

would honor his promise the easy way by waiting
until Lieutenant Price was evacuated back to the
US. If so, Price's men would not get the opportunity to see the lovely Playmate in person.

Marauder ended on January 8. The brigade then

Into the Triangle

DECEPTIVE APPEARANCES: Army training diagram shows how an ordinary-seeming village hootch could hide a squad of armed men or a weapons cache. Frequently these dug-outs linked into a maze of tunnels. Airholes were concealed by vegetation. The enemy used cacti for camouflage because it tended not to wilt and could withstand transplanting.

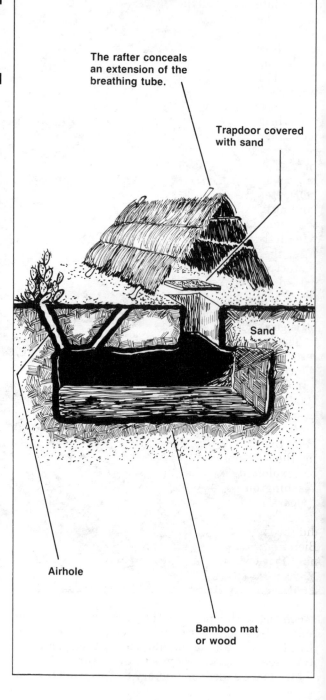

The rafter conceals an extension of the breathing tube.

Trapdoor covered with sand

Sand

Airhole

Bamboo mat or wood

immediately shifted into Operation Crimp. Crimp moved the brigade to the northwest of Saigon. Its mission was a drive through the Ho Bo woods region in Binh Duong province. The object was to destroy the headquarters of the Viet Cong Military Region 4. The 173d was under operational control of the 1st Infantry Division, whose 3d Brigade also took part in the operation.

The brigade command element plus artillery support and armor, cavalry, and engineers moved by road to set up a new fire base and command post. In the now familiar pattern, the three infantry battalions of the 173d executed airmobile assaults in helicopters of the 145th Aviation Battalion into landing zones. They then fanned out on foot to find the enemy.

Brig. Gen. Paul F. Smith — took over command of the 173d as US involvement in Vietnam increased.

In all three assaults, the helicopters were fired on. After the landings, the infantrymen quickly made contact with enemy forces. As the days and nights passed, contact was virtually continuous. However, the 173d's units moved slowly because of the extensive tunnel and bunker systems they found. It did little good to find a tunnel complex and move beyond it. The enemy either remained concealed inside or returned after the friendly unit passed by. The only solution was to pursue him underground.

In Operation Crimp, the brigade's units captured 100 weapons, ranging up to 12.7mm anti-aircraft machine guns. More prosaic, but of greater long-term value, were the enemy documents captured. More than 100,000 pages of documents were found in the various underground headquarters, to be exploited by the analysts in Saigon and Washington.

Operation Crimp ended on January 14. The day before, to the delight of the 173d, *Playboy* magazine did the right thing. Playmate Jo Collins arrived at Bien Hoa. She went to the hospital to present Lieutenant Price with his first issue of the magazine. The 19-year-old Playmate was accompanied by a female chaperone, a photographer, and a writer. The 173d asked Miss Collins to visit as many units as time permitted, and she did. (Her visit was so memorable that the 173d invited her to attend its May 1985 reunion in Washington nearly 20 years later. She did so.)

With Operation Crimp ending, the 173d returned

Into the Triangle

FLUSHING OUT:
Men of A
Company 2/503
use a red
smoke grenade
to flush out a
camouflaged
tunnel system
after discovery
of a concealed
entrance in a
village chief's
yard in the Vo
Dat region.
The smoke
bomb was used
to find
additional
entrances and
reveal
breathing
outlets for
hidden
chambers. As
soon as the
bomb was set
off, troops
would keep
watch for tell-
tale curls of
red smoke
rising from the
ground 50 to
500 meters
away.

Into the Triangle

FIRE SUPPORT: A 105mm howitzer of 3/319 Artillery belches flame in support of the Sky Soldiers during a search-and-destroy sweep into the Hobo Woods during Operation Crimp. New rounds are being set out on the left, empty containers on the right. The 105mm howitzer was light enough to be heli-lifted into the battle zone, had a range of over 11,000 meters and could provide accurate supporting fire on targets only 50 meters ahead of the 173d's own lines.

to base. For the rest of January and into February, smaller company and battalion-sized operations continued. By now the troopers had a saying: "You're either on an operation, returning from one, or leaving for one."

General Williamson's nearly three years in command of the 173d came to an end in late February. He turned the brigade command over to Brigadier General Paul F. Smith. Paul Smith's career included

SP6 Lawrence Joel
—awarded the Medal of Honor for his heroism in 1/503's battle of November 8/9, 1965. Painfully wounded, he injected himself with morphine and insisted on treating other casualties until his evacuation was ordered.

World War II airborne combat as company and battalion commander in the 507th Parachute Infantry, postwar command of the Airborne School Regiment at Fort Benning, and command of the 504th Airborne Battle Group in Germany.

With the change of command, one era closed and a new one began for the Sky Soldiers. A new phase of the war was also under way in the Republic of Vietnam. More US combat troops were arriving.

Airmobile Operations

The Making of an LZ

FROM THE time it had arrived in Vietnam the 173d specialized in difficult quick-reaction missions. For these the Sky Troopers had settled into an efficient combat routine. On notice of an airmobile operation, the squads and platoons formed into five- or six-man groups, the right size load for a Huey. Leaders checked weapons, ammunition, and water. As much of the plan as was known was briefed to the men before liftoff.

Often little detail was known. For instance, if the operation was a quick-reaction mission such as an 'Eagle Flight' to reinforce a unit in contact with the enemy or to exploit a sighting, the men would know only that the helicopters would go into the LZ on a certain compass heading. On landing, they were to move out in a certain direction, reassemble, and follow orders.

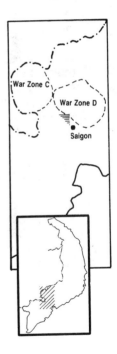

However, deliberate operations planned from the base would start with an intelligence analysis developing a picture of enemy activity and confirming the location of a VC or NVA unit. An operation plan is then made at higher headquarters. The 173d's role is fitted into this overall plan.

The 173d commanders make their own plans to conform to the larger picture. Its battalions and other units do the same. Maps are issued, along with transparent acetate overlays marked with the maneuver and fire support plans.

The plan is outlined to all involved. They prepare their combat loads, draw ammunition, and check their equipment. Troopers going out for the first time wonder how they will behave under fire. Veterans wonder if they'll get hit this time, or if they'll make it through one more combat assault uninjured. The 'short-timers,' men whose rotation date is

Airmobile Operations

THE SWARM: An eight-ship formation of Hueys, UH-1D helicopters from the 335 Aviation (The Cowboys), rushes more than half a company of Sky Troopers into a newly created LZ. The blackened and shattered tree stumps are all that is left of the jungle canopy destroyed by heavy bombardment to create the LZ.

near, think about getting through the operation and back to the States.

At the appointed time, the units break up into their helicopter loads. The approaching lift helicopters are heard before they are seen. The wop-wop-wop of their rotors beating the air rises in frequency as they draw near. In a column they look like

a swarm of disciplined dragonflies as they approach.
The troopers are on their feet. Leaders hold their
maps tight to keep them from blowing away in the
rotor downwash. Weapons safety catches are on so
some idiot doesn't put a round through an engine.

The troopers climb aboard, settling on the
diamond-patterned aluminum floor. There are no

Staff Sgt. Charles B. Morris —awarded both the Distinguished Service Cross and the Medal of Honor by President Lyndon B. Johnson. Sgt. Morris received the nation's highest honor for his courage and determination in an eight-hour firefight in June 1966. Wounded four times in the course of battle he continued to lead his men as he engaged the enemy, throwing grenades and firing his rifle one-handed until relief arrived.

seats. Door gunners pat their M-60 machine guns reassuringly.

The commander of the helicopters radios an order. The helicopter pilots bring up engine power. On command, they lift their birds to a low hover, about three feet off the ground. The leader radios the order to go. The pilots lower the helicopter noses and gain airspeed. They climb to cruise altitude, about 1,200 feet.

The helicopter doors are off. The wind whips through the troop compartment. The scenery below might be rice land, with the turtleback pattern of dikes. Or it could be primary jungle, with the canopy tops reaching 200 feet into the air. Or it might be the coastal plain or Delta, with streams sluggishly flowing in a pattern like the veins on the back of your hand. Old B-52 bomb craters often have water in their bottoms. They look like suburban swimming pools in South Florida or California, without the houses.

Nearing the landing zone the pilots might pass back a comment to the door gunners about the smoke from artillery and air strikes hitting around the LZ. The door gunners relay information to the troops. But the troops can hear better than the crew, because they have no headsets or earphones. They listen for the crump of bombs bursting in the soil, the whoosh of gunship rockets, and for the staccato stuttering of machine guns on fighters and gunships both. They watch for the F-100 and F-4 fighters, as they roll off the target and climb to position for another pass. Now and then a fighter flies the wrong way. He sails through the helicopter formation, leaving momentary terror in his wake.

Some LZs can take a dozen or more Hueys, the bulk of a rifle company. Others may be smaller. Allowing clearance between blades and fuselages, and distance for a steep approach and climb, a two-ship LZ needs a space about 30 by 60 meters.

The smaller the LZ, the longer the helicopters are exposed to enemy fire.

The landing zone might be 'cold,' with no enemy fire. Or the enemy might resist the landing. Then the LZ is 'hot.' A hot LZ can turn into an awful mess in a hurry if helicopters are hit and downed. Then everyone must keep his head to make the operation work. Gunships pour fire around the edges of a hot

LZ. The helicopter door gunners fire both to left and right, pouring 7.62mm machine gun rounds into the trees to keep the enemy's heads down. Commanders and observers search for the flash of enemy weapons, then direct fire on them.

Like all commanders of the 173d, General Smith was always present in his command chopper in the air over an assault landing. With him were an operations officer, an artillery representative, and a member of the brigade's air section. Each had his own radio to deal with his portion of the action. The airborne commander had the flexibility of the helicopter and reach of communications "to get things back on track in a hurry," General Smith recalls.

"When the command chopper began running low on fuel it was replaced by another. The brigade's deputy commander and a similar coordinating team were aboard to take charge. These two groups rotated as necessary so that the capability of spotting glitches and overcoming them was immediate." The same procedure was used for extracting units by helicopter, which General Smith describes as "infinitely more hairy than insertions."

A cold LZ is a pleasure to watch. For a few moments it is transformed from a quiet clearing in the jungle into a disciplined and busy air terminal. Colored smoke marks the spot for the lead helicopter, and the formation homes on it. The formation descends. The helicopters touch down in column (or vee or line abreast, as required), settling on the skids again. The pilots keep power up and ready to lift. The troops pile off the helicopters, hitching up their rucksacks and equipment. They dash away in the direction briefed. If that is to the right, the men pouring out of the left sides of the helicopters run around the noses of their birds. No one passes a helicopter by its tail. The tail rotor can decapitate you in a split second.

If the ground is soft, it sucks against the men's jungle boots, slowing them down. If they have landed in elephant grass, it saws across their faces and arms; if wet rice fields, they face the choice of running along the dikes where the going is easy, or through the fields where the mud and water slow them down. On the dikes, in a tight column, they are easy targets for enemy fire. So they slog. That

Viet Cong booby traps were a constant danger. After a survey showed that more than half the mines were detonated by unwary infantrymen, a school of Tunnels and Mines was established at Cu Chi, and boot camps in the States started including ambush and booby trap detection in their training.

This nail bomb detonated by a tripwire was typical of the devices faced by US foot soldiers.

Airmobile Operations

HOT RECEPTION:
A troop commander's eye view of an assault landing on a hot LZ. Colored smoke from signal grenades and fires still smoldering from preparatory artillery bombardments and airstrikes mark out the LZ. If the battalion staff has calculated correctly, the enemy around the LZ will be out of action at the moment the Hueys touch down.

never changes. The squad leaders count their men, place them into the movement formation, and report them ready to the platoon leaders. The platoon leaders radio their readiness to the company commander. He speads out his command group. The forward observers, forward air controllers, and the company's own radiotelephone operators spread out. The company commander gives the word to move out.

The point men in each squad watch, smell, and listen for the enemy. Everyone listens for the *swiiissssssh* of incoming mortar rounds, or the cracksnap of enemy rifle fire. Their stomachs tighten up in anticipation and the sweat rolls down their faces and necks in the close humid heat. An olive drab towel around their necks absorbs the sweat.

When the company arrives at the designated spot, it may be time to eat. Security outposts are placed 50 - 75 meters in all directions. When the word comes to move again, the outposts are pulled in, the squads form in the movement formation, and the process is repeated.

This may go on for days with no enemy contact.

STEADY, BOY: A German shepherd and his handler on brigade base perimeter patrol. The 39th Scout Dog Platoon was a welcome addition to the 173d. In the closed-in jungle terrain of Vietnam a dog's keen sense of smell could prove a lifesaver. The dogs were trained to detect the Viet Cong by scent. Anyone who had been in a chemically defoliated area was immediately recognizable. To disguise their scent as friendly, the VC took to washing with US Army soap bought on the black market.

The leaders and men must guard against becoming complacent, especially at night. The entrenching tool, a portable folding shovel carried by every man, is vital then. Swinging their trenching tools, the troops dig into the protection of the ground for the night. Night security is posted. Half the men sleep, wrapped up in ponchos. The other half remain on alert, waiting out the night.

On some occasions there was no time for complacency, as the 2d Battalion, 503d Infantry, found on Operation Silver City on March 16, 1966, as it swept part of War Zone D. In the previous four days they had made contact with small groups of VC in the dense jungle. The night of March 15 - 16, the battalion had taken up a defensive perimeter as usual. On the morning of March 16, a patrol from Company B began to move out into the jungle. About the same time, a resupply helicopter was descending into the LZ within the perimeter, only 75 meters across.

Suddenly, heavy enemy fire hit the helicopter. It crashed into the perimeter. With that, heavy enemy fire erupted in a circle around the 2d Battalion's position. Company B's patrol was caught in the murderous fire. The enemy followed with assaults supported by automatic weapons, mortars, and artillery. Leaves and chunks of wood flew, ripped from the trees by bullets and shell fragments.

A heavy VC attack smashed at the boundary between Companies A and C. The assault was pressed at pointblank range. Everyone fought, including the wounded. Artillery dropped the 105mm rounds against the rear of the enemy, exploding only a couple of hundred meters in front of the position. The attack broke up. The men, bloody and sweat-soaked, redistributed ammunition and waited for the next assault.

It came soon, pressing against the center and left flank of Company B. Again the enemy attacked in coordinated waves, supported by mortars and artillery. The paratroopers of Company B had their night holes to fight from. They dug deeper, their perimeter held steady.

The enemy kept up steady fire around the perimeter. He regrouped and concentrated his forces. Then he attacked the flank of Company C. The VC poured in heavy preparatory fire, followed by waves of screaming infantry. The paratroopers prevailed.

Brig. Gen. John R. Deane, Jr. —took over command of the 173d in December 1966 a month after being awarded the Distinguished Service Cross for gallantry during Operation Attleboro. Later a task force would be named after him.

Airmobile Operations

HOT SHIP: Airview of close support. A USAF F-100 Super Sabre, twin napalm tanks under its wings, banks over the Mekong Delta in preparation for a second bombing run over target. The two-seat fighter bomber was a vital part of LZ operations. Capable of carrying up to 6,000 lbs. of ordnance, the F-100 could be used to first clear the area and then provide cover with strafing attacks on enemy positions.

The enemy attacks waned, then finally stopped. The battalion held firm in its perimeter, an epic stand.

After the battle, documents and other intelligence confirmed that the entire Viet Cong 271st Main Force Regiment, reinforced by two VC artillery battalions, had attacked 2/503. A total of 303 enemy bodies littered the ground around the perimeter.

The Australian and New Zealand contingent was not destined to stay with the 173d, so a third airborne infantry battalion was activated back at Fort

Campbell on April 1, 1966. It was designated 4th Battalion, 503d Infantry. The battalion joined the 173d on June 25.

Soon after Operation Attleboro, General Smith was promoted to major general. Although the 173d was a brigadier general's command, General Westmoreland left him in command until calling him to Saigon in December.

General Smith turned over command of the 173d on December 28 to Brigadier General John R.

Deane, Jr. A 1942 West Point graduate, he knew many of the officers and noncoms of the 173d. Most recently, Deane had been assistant division commander of the 1st Infantry Division. He had earned the Distinguished Service Cross for gallantry during Operation Attleboro.

The next major operation for the 173d was Cedar Falls, which took them back into the Iron Triangle in a combined armor/infantry search and destroy mission. It was not an operation marked by massive clashes with the enemy, and the troopers of the 173d again turned into 'tunnel rats' and document scavengers. Cedar Falls paid off in the rich haul of documents and enemy supplies uncovered in the

Airmobile Operations

AIR SUPPLY LINE: Heavily laden with ammo, grenades and their dismantled mortar, a section of Sky Troopers move off a muddy LZ after airborne re-supply on a jungle search and destroy patrol in Phuc Tuy province. Every man carried four one-pound grenades. Nicknamed 'baseballs,' these smooth-skinned grenades shattered on detonation into 1,000 tiny pieces that could kill or maim over a 10-meter radius.

maze of the Iron Triangle's fortifications, head-quarters, and supporting installations. More than 500,000 pages of documents were captured. Among them was a prize seized by Company C, 2d Bn, 503d. They killed a courier who was carrying the codes for the VC's Military Region IV headquarters. As a direct result a high official of MR IV was captured not long after.

With the end of Cedar Falls, War Zones C and D and the Iron Triangle fell temporarily silent. The lull would last less than two weeks. Now the stage was set for the multidivision 'big operation' General Westmoreland had been planning for some time: Junction City.

63

Junction City

The First Combat Jump

A COMBAT parachute jump is the ultimate satisfaction and test for paratroopers. From the time the 173d Airborne Brigade was committed in Vietnam in 1965, its airborne troopers expected that eventually they would jump into combat by parachute, as their predecessors did in World War II and Korea.

They were to be disappointed for nearly two years. From 1965 into early 1967, the brigade led the way in airmobile assaults. But they used helicopters, not parachutes, to leapfrog terrain and time barriers. Partly this was because no real parachute assault situations materialized. Also, by using its own helicopters the Army retained control of combat airlift to the fighting units. It did not have to ask the Air Force for use of its fixed-wing cargo airplanes.

Still the notion of a mass parachute assault was attractive to General Westmoreland. In response to his pointed enquiries, in October 1966 subordinate commanders prepared several proposals for battalion jumps in the border areas.

The 173d was directed to ready a battalion-size task force to go into specialist training for a possible parachute assault. General Paul F. Smith selected the 2d Battalion, 503d Infantry, commanded by Lieutenant Colonel Robert H. Sigholtz, as the key element of the task force. Besides the airborne infantry battalion the task force included Battery A, 319th Field Artillery (with six 105mm howitzers), an engineer squad, a military police squad, a radio research team, an interrogation team, elements of the brigade headquarters to form a tactical command post, and combat support elements from the brigade's support battalion.

Sigholtz's battalion slogan was: "We Try Harder,"

borrowed from the Avis car rental company. It had sent him hundreds of its red and white buttons, in English and several other languages.

With Operation Junction City, the opportunity came for a one-battalion parachute assault by his task force. The drop zone: a wide clearing in the jungle near a crossroads hamlet called Katum, six kilometers from the Cambodian border, and about 42 kilometers north of Tay Ninh City.

Katum's location close to the Cambodian border made High Command's intelligence officers consider it one of the favored sites for the top enemy headquarters in South Vietnam: COSVN, the Central Office for South Vietnam. If it could be found and eliminated, Hanoi's timetable would be set back by years.

Locating and destroying COSVN was a major goal of the grand plan for Operation Junction City. It was also intended to trap and destroy subordinate enemy headquarters and units in War Zone C.

The operation would be conducted in two phases. Phase I would begin on February 22. In the western part of War Zone C, five US brigades would form a horseshoe-shaped cordon, with the open end pointing down toward the south. On the second day, two

COMBAT DROP: This is how it looks when you leap into battle from a C-130. As he jumps the paratrooper counts 'One thousand, two thousand, three thousand, four thousand'; as he completes the count, there is a sudden tug and the T-10 chute opens. The picture of Drop Zone Charlie (right) was issued to aid aerial recognition. The white rectangle covers an area 1,150 feet wide by 6,000 feet long and shows the assembly area for 2/503s A, B, and C companies.

forces would drive from the south into the open end of the horseshoe.

The 173d was given an area on the northeast curve of the horseshoe. General Deane's Sky Troopers were to assault by parachute and helicopter into the fight. Katum was about midway in the 173d's assigned front.

On February 11, Sigholtz got the word: the 2d Battalion task force's combat jump was on. To keep secrecy, only he and Major Don Phillips, his operations officer did the planning, and on February 21, the day before the drop, the 780-man airborne task force was placed in quarantine at Camp Zinn near Bien Hoa. Sigholtz briefed the men on the mission. He said later, "To a man, the word was received with great jubilation."

The same day the heavy equipment loads were rigged. For firepower, the loads included the six 105mm howitzers of Battery A, 3d Battalion, 319th Artillery and 2,400 rounds of ammunition; six of 2/503's own 81mm mortars and 1,500 rounds; four 4.2-inch mortars and 746 rounds. Vehicles rigged for drop were four .75-ton trucks, five jeeps and one trailer, and six of the M274 'Mule' vehicles. (The Mule was a small, low-slung cart with a gasoline

Lt. Col. Robert Sigholtz— task force commander for the jump. A 'We Try Harder' button is pinned to his shirt collar. When the Avis car rental company heard that the battalion had adopted their slogan they sent the troops hundreds of buttons.

engine that could carry up to half a ton of cargo, specially designed for airborne units.)

At Camp Zinn, the paratroopers were awakened and fed in the middle of the night. At 0530 hours, the men and their equipment loaded into trucks for the short ride to Bien Hoa and the C-130 transports. Guides led the men through the darkness to their designated aircraft.

As the sky in the east began to lighten, the men could see the nearly full moon setting on the western

Junction City

GO!

The moment of truth for para- troopers. Lt. Col. Sigholtz has just leapt from the left- hand door of this C-130 transport. Next to make the 1,000-ft. jump is Sgt. Maj. Harold Proffitt, followed by the command group's radio telephone operator, Cpl. Shadlee.

For a minute the task force was effectively leaderless as the three jumped.

The jump was successful. The 778-man force suffered no chute failures and only 11 minor injuries.

horizon. Now the Sky Soldiers put on their para- chutes and equipment for the real thing. The over- night low temperature was 72 degrees. It felt good. As the sun rose, the men sweated and grunted as they tightened the belly band and leg straps of their T-10 main parachutes to the hurting point. Men helped each other hook on the T-7A reserve parachute. Together, the two parachutes added near- ly 40 pounds to the troopers' loads. When 'chuted up, the paratroopers looked like a horde of pregnant hunchbacked beetles, waddling around humped partly over, groaning under the weight of their parachutes, weapons, ammunition, water, and personal equipment.

Each man checked himself and was checked by his leaders and buddies.

Bien Hoa air base was noisy as ever, with the earsplitting roar of F-4 Phantom and F-100 Super Sabre fighters taking off. The paratroopers were quiet, however, as jumpmasters completed their final checks. They were especially attentive to the four anchor line cables stretching down the fuselage of each C-130. Those were the cables to which the paratroopers hooked up their static lines. (The static line pulls the parachute open when the man leaps out the door.)

Parachute riggers carefully prepare crates of artillery ammunition for dropping into forward areas.

The kerosene smell of jet fuel permeated the air at Bien Hoa. The men felt their skin getting warm and the sweat starting to roll as the sun rose higher in the sky.

The first troop-laden aircraft took off at 0825 hours. All 13 were airborne in three minutes. The aircraft reached the drop zone after a short flight over a dogleg route in absolute radio silence.

As the formation neared the drop zone, the crew in the lead aircraft could see the smoke rising and hear the explosions from the final preparatory air strikes. An airborne forward air controller marked the drop zone with colored smoke, confirming its location to the navigators in the aircraft. Each navigator determined his own airplane's alignment and exact time of release. Jumpmasters leaned out the doors of their aircraft to check the route. Inside the aircraft, the jumpers were crammed into their seats, bulging with the bulk of their two parachutes, weapons, and equipment.

Five minutes from Drop Zone Charlie they were ordered to their feet for the final routine of harness checks. In keeping with long tradition, each jumpmaster yelled, "ARE YOU READY?" The men yelled back in unison, "HELL, YES!"

The jumpmaster gave the command: "STAND IN THE DOOR." The first man at each door pivoted, released the static line he had been holding, planted his leading foot on the doorsill, and slapped his hands firmly on the outside edges of the jump door. The feel of the cool prop blast was welcome on their hands and faces. They watched the shining red light, waiting for the moment when it would go off and the green jump light come on—the signal to leap into space. Now the men were ready. They stamped their feet and yelled encouragement to each other as the moment to drop came near.

As each plane neared the calculated drop point, each navigator uncovered the switch that controlled the green jump light. At the drop point, the navigator flipped off the red light. It was jump time.

When the green jump light flashed in the lead plane, 173d commander, General 'Uncle Jack' Deane, led the troops out of the right-hand door. Colonel Sigholtz led out of the left-hand door. The rest of the men in the first pass stomped down the aisle, turned into the doors, and jumped after Deane and Sigholtz into the warm morning sky. The men shouted: "ONE THOUSAND, TWO THOUSAND, THREE THOUSAND, FOUR THOUSAND," and waited for the opening shock which meant their T-10 parachute had worked.

Sigholtz and Deane leaped right on schedule at 0900. The C-130s following their aircraft flew across Drop Zone Charlie at 130 knots, spaced at 20-second intervals.

The troopers had less than a minute hanging in the air to orient themselves with the drop zone and to pick out their own assembly areas on the ground. The task force used colored smoke grenades and colored helium balloons released by the first jumpers on the ground as markers. Colored tape on helmet covers matched the colored smoke and balloons of the assembly areas.

The jumpers from the first pass began landing on target. When they smacked into the ground, they rolled onto their feet, then scrambled out of the parachute harness, grabbed weapons and equipment, and ran to their assembly points. The object: to assemble men of the task force from a bunch of C-130 passengers into fighting combat units. The assembly went rapidly, since no opposition developed.

After crossing the drop zone the aircraft stream turned sharply to the right, remained at drop altitude of 1,000 feet, and returned to the previous track for a second pass necessitated by the small size of the DZ. The jump was complete at 0910. Out of

Gen. William Westmoreland —the US commander in Vietnam. He wanted to watch the jump from overhead but was sent to the fake drop zone. By the time the mistake was discovered it was too late.

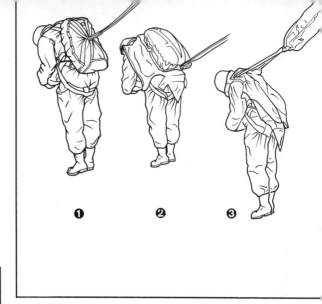

① **②** **③**

a total of 778 troops only 11 men sustained minor injuries.

At 0930, right on time and on target, the ten heavy drop C-130s appeared in trail formation. The drop went smoothly and without mishap.

By 1000, all men and equipment of the task force were deployed on the ground, the brigade command post was functioning, and the artillery fire support base was ready to deliver fire. Patrols moved out to search the area, cocky with the confidence of airborne troops who have landed safely once again and in whose veins the adrenaline is still pumping.

A visitor to the brigade command post in late morning commented on the combined sense of euphoria and lassitude he observed in many of the men who had jumped. The euphoria was the good feeling that always comes from a successful jump. The lassitude was the result of having had a strong shot of adrenaline in the buildup to the jump, followed by the 'coming down' reaction after the drop.

The drop was unopposed. The enemy in the vicinity was either avoiding contact or was occupied with the troops of the 1st and 25th Infantry divisions, the 11th Armored Cavalry, the 196th Light Infantry Brigade, and other US and South Vietnamese units. They had begun surging over the area from first light, saturating the skies with helicopters.

General Westmoreland wanted to watch the

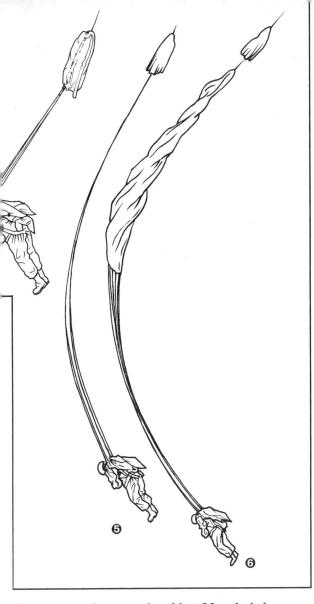

Junction City

HOW A PARACHUTE OPENS:

❶ The static line pulls out the fastening in the centre of the backpack; ❷ the elastic bands pull clear, ❸ allowing the main chute in its deployment bag to lift off; ❹ the paratrooper falls into a face-down position (as the suspension lines begin to extend he is pulled back upright and the bag comes off); ❺ & ❻ the canopy starts to fill with air. The static line is connected to the top of the parachute by a weaker break cord, which snaps when the canopy is pulled clear. It all takes less than four seconds.

Katum jump from overhead but Murphy's law was at work, and he was sent the coordinates of the fake drop zone.

An hour after 2/503's jump, helicopters were available for reinforcement. Its sister units, 1/503 and 4/503, made combat assaults by helicopter into four landing zones nearby.

The blocking forces were now all in position. The

opening acts of Junction City had gone smoothly. As far as the 173d was concerned it was a sign of things to come.

Although the brigade remained in the combat area for nearly two months no major contacts with the enemy were made.

The VC main force chose to fight on only a few occasions. COSVN was not found; it had apparently withdrawn into its sanctuary in Cambodia. Looking

Junction City

GETTING CLOSE: Paratroopers hit the dirt as they make contact with the enemy during Operation Junction City. Although a large-scale operation, Junction City was a succession of small-unit firefights for the Sky Soldiers as the enemy avoided contact. Behind them they left valuable information. In one underground bunker the 173d discovered a complete Viet Cong propaganda center equipped with printing presses.

back at Cedar Falls and Junction City, the senior commanders realized that in both cases there were not enough troops to run the operations and then stay in the areas to prevent the VC from returning. General Bernard Rogers, then Assistant Division Commander of the 1st Infantry Division, said, "In neither instance were we able to stay around, and it was not long before there was evidence of the enemy's return."

The Road to Battle

The Move to the Central Highlands

IN LATE MAY 1967, the 173d continued to operate in the area east and northeast of Saigon. That phase of its existence ended on May 24. The brigade was alerted to move once again. It was to fly back to Pleiku in the Central Highlands. The 173d would join in Operation Francis Marion, then a 4th Infantry Division show.

The Sky Troopers had been to Pleiku nearly two years earlier, and had found the cooler climate in the highlands a welcome change from the steamy lowlands.

Within 24 hours, the brigade began flying out of Bien Hoa in USAF C-130s. Twenty-one aircraft were used for the lift, making 208 flights to carry the bulk of the troops and their equipment into the highlands.

Now under operational control of the 4th Infantry Division, the brigade set up its command post at Catecka, 2,400 feet above sea level and about 12 kilometers south of Pleiku.

General Deane deployed his battalions searching south of Catecka and fanning out into the Ia Drang valley. The 1st Cavalry Division (Airmobile) had fought hard battles in the Ia Drang in October and November 1965, but this time the NVA forces avoided contact.

They were, however, applying pressure against the chain of Special Forces camps farther north.

The camps were manned by ethnic tribesmen of the Civilian Irregular Defense Groups (CIDG), advised by men of the US Army's Special Forces. The camps were situated in key locations along invasion and resupply routes all along the border areas. They were remote in every sense. Resupply was usually by air. For immediate fire support, they had their own mortars and nothing else. US Army divisions

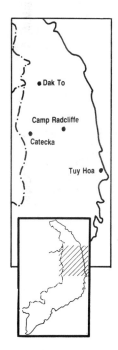

The Road
to Battle

ROUGH FIELD:
Chaplain
Charles J.
Watters
(center) of
2/503 and his
assistant keep
their heads
down as they
move off a
hastily
prepared LZ
during
Operation
Francis Marion
near Pleiku in
June 1967.
The 191-day
operation in
the western
portion of the
Central
Highlands
resulted in over
1,200 enemy
casualties.

were usually given the missions of going to the relief of the CIDG camps in dire cases. But in reality, the CIDG troops and their Special Forces advisers had to rely on their own patrolling and preparations to get warning of an attack and to ride it out until help could arrive.

In mid-June 1967, CIDG patrols and others made contact with NVA troops not far from Dak To, 80 kilometers north of Catecka. To the intelligence analysts, it looked as if the North Vietnamese were moving in to attack the camp at Dak To and the nearby town of Tan Canh, where an ARVN regiment was based. As usual, the 173d was alerted to

head to the scene. The operation was dubbed Greeley. An advance party flew to Dak To on June 16. They arrived in time to undergo a mortar attack on the Special Forces camp that night.

On the 17th, the Sky Troopers began flying into Dak To airstrip. The Air Force marveled at the Army's ability to extract its forces from active operations in one place, proceed to the nearest C-130 airstrip, load up, and move to another place to fight again. To the Sky Troopers, such movements were now routine, another part of its lengthening history.

The C-130 pilots had to thread into the east - west strip at Dak To under lowering ceilings and wisps

The Road to Battle

FIELD SERVICE:
With upturned ammo boxes for an altar and a chasuble cut from camouflage material, Padre Watters says Mass at a 2/503 Fire Support Base near Pleiku in June 1967. Soon he was to be at the side of his congregation as they fought for their lives.

of cloud that clung to the mountains rising to more than 4,000 feet on both sides.

Part of the brigade moved by motor convoy from Catecka through Pleiku, then Kontum, and into Dak To.

The main body was reassembled near the CIDG camp and ready to go on the 18th.

The threats to the Dak To forces were expected to materialize either from the enemy building up to the southwest or from his forces in the hills to the northeast. Consequently, the 173d had to prepare against both.

Brig. Gen. Leo H. Schweiter —took control of the 173d in time for the airlift to Tuy Hoa.

The 2/503 Infantry started operating south of Dak To on June 18. It headed south for four days, then turned back toward Dak To. While it was out, the NVA commander had begun moving a battalion into the area. This was not known to the US force, which set up nighttime defensive perimeters on a ridge for the night of June 21 - 22.

On the morning of June 22, the 2/503 began moving out slowly through the dense foliage. Company A was in the lead, followed by Companies C and B.

The point platoon of Company A, 2d Battalion, 503d Infantry, ran into the flank of the 24th NVA Regiment. It was an elite formation that had just crossed the border from Laos, estimated to be 800 strong. The first NVA spotted were in khaki uniforms with berets on their heads. The second platoon of Company A crashed forward to reinforce the point. By then the NVA troops were firing from both flanks as well as the front. The remainder of Company A could not make it to the beleaguered platoons, and was forced back into Company C. Heavy artillery and air strikes were called down on the NVA attackers.

In a battle fought face-to-face in the misty hills, Company A fought off two human wave attacks. In a third attack its position was overrun and the company badly mauled. It suffered 76 killed and 22 wounded. Friendly artillery and gunships could not check the repeated assaults, although they were reported to have killed more than 400 of the NVA attackers. (The survivors discount this figure.)

Companies B and C were sent in relief. The enemy fire repulsed them on the afternoon of June 22. They did not reach the survivors of Company A until the

J.BATCHELOR

SECOND STICK

A Hercules C-130 transport makes a second pass at 1,000-feet over Drop Zone Charlie at the outset of Operation Junction City. Each man had just one minute in the air—just time enough to orient himself towards the coloured smoke grenade that acted as a marker for his company's assembly area.

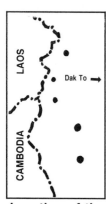

Location of the Special Forces camps defended by the 173d against the NVA incursions across the Laotian border.

the following morning. The NVA had stripped the dead troopers of their gear.

After the battle, General Westmoreland told the 2d Battalion that the gallant stand by Company A had prevented the enemy from overrunning the camp at Dak To. Survivors recall his saying they had just won a great battle, and remember wondering if he was talking about the same bloody fight they had just gone through.

The brigade next fought north and northwest of Dak To, against the building threats to the camps at Dak Pek and Dak Seang, making contact occasionally with the NVA forces in the area as the summer passed.

On August 24, General Deane turned over command of the 173d to Brigadier General Leo H. Schweiter. General Schweiter had a long airborne background. During World War II, he had made combat jumps in Normandy and Holland as a member of the 101st Airborne Division. He participated in the Inchon landing, and later commanded a regiment in combat in Korea. He had also commanded a battle group of the 82d Airborne Division, and the 5th Special Forces Group (Airborne). He joined the 173d from duty as Assistant Divison Commander of the 101st Airborne Division.

In mid-September, Schweiter was told to move the 173d again. The 1st and 4th battalions of the 503d Infantry were airlifted to the seacoast near Tuy Hoa in Phu Yen Province. For the moment 2/503 was left in the highlands under control of the 4th Infantry Division.

It took three days for the Air Force to lift the main body of the brigade from Dak To to Tuy Hoa. The Dak To airstrip deteriorated rapidly, potholes blooming daily under heavy rains and the pounding of C-130 tires. The engineers patched the runway as quickly as it fell apart, and when the main body was lifted out, did a complete repair job. Having an operable airstrip at Dak To was essential, because the NVA build-up to the west was accelerating. In Tuy Hoa, the mission of the 173d in Operation Bolling was to destroy VC and NVA forces in the area, and to protect the rice harvest. In this operation its armored company, D Company 16th Armor, was especially useful. It secured the roads and moved rapidly across country, keeping the enemy off

The Road to Battle

FIRE SUPPORT:
A member of a 4.2in. mortar crew hangs a round at the top of a tube, waiting for the command; "FIRE!" at a fire support base in the Central Highlands. The weapon is elevated for near-maximum range — about 4.5 miles for a 20 lb. bomb, which, unusually for a mortar, is spin-stabilised for accuracy by the rifled barrel.

The Road to Battle

FIRE CALL: A 3/503d platoon leader calls in artillery on a VC ambush. The radio telephone antenna is bent over the operator's shoulder to avoid snagging on low branches, hampering movement and betraying his position. Officer and RTO routinely faced in opposite directions to keep an all-round look-out.

balance. It was while the 173d operated around Tuy Hoa that its fourth infantry battalion joined.

Designated as the 3d Battalion, 503d Infantry, the battalion was activated at Fort Bragg, North Carolina, in May. It trained for five months then flew to join the brigade in October in the middle of Operation Bolling. About the same time, the brigade moved its base from the old stand at Bien Hoa, its home for two and one-half years. The new base was established at Camp Radcliff at An Khe.

Late in October, the situation around Dak To was becoming more serious. Hard evidence mounted to confirm that the NVA was massing its regiments. The Air Force lifted the 173d back into Dak To

during the first week of November. By now the mixture of rain, mist, and low cloud known as the 'crachin' complicated the airlift. As the Air Force lifted the 173d back into Dak To it also flew in reinforcements from the 1st Cavalry Division and ARVN units. The airstrip was a messy place. Trucks drove on or next to it because there were no roads leading to it; bulldozers and C-130s collided; and uncontrolled swarms of helicopters complicated the task of flying. With the airlift back into Dak To, the 173d once more had three battalions ready to fight: the 1st, 2d, and 4th of the 503d. The 3d Battalion and Company D, 16th Armor, continued Operation Bolling around Tuy Hoa. The stage was set for high drama.

Dak To and Hill 875

The Border Battles

BY NOVEMBER 1967, the US High Command felt optimistic about the progress of the war. At home, however, opposition continued to swell as the war dragged on. General Westmoreland flew back to the United States in mid-month. He had been summoned to report to President Johnson and the Congress, and, as he saw it, for public relations purposes.

One of his first stops in Washington was a ceremony at the White House on November 16, where he saw President Johnson present the Medal of Honor to one of the 173d's Sky Troopers, Staff Sergeant Charles B. Morris of Company A, 2d Battalion, 503d Infantry. He had earned the Medal on June 29, 1966. Three more Medals of Honor would be earned by 173d Sky Troopers during Westmoreland's visit to Washington. All would be awarded posthumously.

Westmoreland spoke optimistically about the war before the National Press Club on November 21. He told the audience that the war was moving into 'Phase Three.' He defined that as continuing to destroy the enemy while building up the Vietnamese armed forces. He said in Phase Four, US units would begin to turn more of the work over to the Vietnamese and start to withdraw.

While Westmoreland was in Washington, however, intense fighting had developed around the Special Forces camp at Dak To. Even as he gave the speech at the Press Club, 2/503 was in a fight for survival, with the outcome not certain. It was the latest in a series of battles around Dak To.

That fight and two others (at Song Be and Loc Ninh) became known as the 'border battles.'

To the 173d, they became an epic, and Dak To a place where scores of its paratroopers were killed in

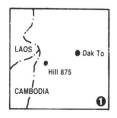

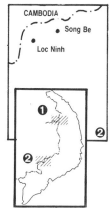

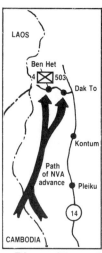

Disposition of N. Vietnamese and US forces west of Dak To as of November 2, 1967. The NVA forces numbered 4,292. The 4/503 had 515 men.

a fierce battle at close quarters in the mists and dark foliage of the highland jungles. It created memories in red and green. Red for the blood that flowed from men on both sides and for the flash of tracers and explosions of mortars, artillery, and bombs. Green for the trees and brush, camouflage, and equipment.

Near the end of October 1967, intelligence reports built up a picture of a North Vietnamese division consisting of five regiments moving toward Dak To. An NVA defector said the Special Forces camps there and at Ben Het were its objectives.

The US 4th Infantry Division was responsible for the area. Its commander, Major General William R. Peers, began moving extra US and Vietnamese battalions into the mountains. As the units moved into the hills, contacts with the enemy increased in number and size. The developing situation confirmed the enemy strength. Prudence dictated reinforcement. The 173d was committed to the mission.

The area where the brigade was committed lies about 20 kilometers west of the camp at Dak To. The mountains in the area range up to 1,900 meters high. They are interlaced with river valleys and streams. Continuous double and triple jungle canopy ranging to 100 - 200 feet covers the mountains. The weather during the period was excellent, near the end of the dry season in that region. Daily high and low temperatures were 91 and 55 degrees.

As the situation developed, intelligence reports confirmed the presence of the 1st North Vietnamese Army (NVA) Division. Its regiments (their strength in parentheses): the 32d (1,337), 66th (1,335), and 24th (1,620); and the 40th NVA Artillery Regiment.

The 4th Battalion, 503d Infantry, commanded by Lieutenant Colonel James H. Johnson, was ordered west from Dak To on November 2 to meet the threat to the camp at Ben Het. It carried 515 men on its rolls. On November 3 and 4, other battalions of the 4th Infantry Division encountered the 32d NVA Regiment in a series of sharp fights. It seemed to the intelligence analysts that the NVA forces had changed their plans because of the rapid American response. They speculated that the NVA were going to ground in positions already prepared, instead of moving against the camps, as was thought earlier. So the decision was made to move against the enemy to destroy as many of his men as possible. Colonel

Dak To and Hill 875

BATTLE LOAD:
A Sky Soldier went into battle as heavily laden as a pack mule. The rucksack, stuffed, carried basic equipment and weighed up to 50 lbs. In addition, he carried three days' rations, 500 rounds of M-16 rifle ammunition, four fragmentation and two smoke grenades, one or more Claymore mines, 200 rounds for the M-60 machine gun, and three canteens of water. He also had his individual weapon: an M-16 rifle or M-79 grenade launcher.

Unofficial issue —a Sky Trooper on perimeter guard keeps his shotgun at the ready. Although the M-16 was standard issue the units requested—and received— shotguns. In the close-quarter fighting in the densely wooded hills around Dak To a shotgun with its wide spread of shot was often the ideal weapon.

Johnson's 4/503 moved out from Ben Het toward a hill about seven kilometers southwest, where the enemy was expected to be found.

As usual, the paratroopers went into battle heavily laden. The rucksack carried each man's basic equipment and clothing, and weighed about 50 pounds. In addition, the men each carried three days' rations, 500 rounds of M-16 rifle ammunition, four fragmentation and two smoke grenades, one or more Claymore mines, 200 rounds for the M-60 machine gun, and three canteens of water. Every man also had his individual weapon: an M-16 rifle or M-79 grenade launcher. The M-60 machine gunners carried nearly 2,000 additional rounds, plus the gun and their own gear.

Before the unit reached its objective, it was decided to move the artillery closer to the scene of combat. Hill 823 was selected as the place to set up a fire support base. On November 6, the fourth day of slogging along, Companies A and D were moving in column towards the southwest, with D about 1,500 meters ahead. Company D's lead platoon found an enemy communications wire and followed it up a hill called Ngok Kom Leat.

In short order, the company was hit hard by NVA regulars. Captain Thomas H. Baird, the commander, pulled his 85 men into a defensive perimeter, and called on air strikes and artillery support. Friendly air was not available, but the 3/319 began to hit the hill with high explosive rounds from its six 105mm howitzers.

Captain Baird was wounded early in the fight but remained in command. His outposts pulled back into the perimeter under sniper fire from NVA soldiers in the trees. An air strike by F-100s dropping bombs and napalm and firing machine guns enabled Baird to establish his perimeter. Just in time, because the NVA began attacking in platoon force on three sides of Company D's tight little oval. The fight was fierce and at close range, wearing on for three hours as the afternoon passed. Company D held on, and was joined by a squad from Company A, moving ahead of the main body. The enemy still held the top of the hill. Company D hung on about two-thirds of the way up. Helicopter gunships, air strikes, and the 3/319 artillery pounded the hilltop, keeping the NVA from renewing their attacks. At about the same time that Company D was engaged (early afternoon), Company B was being lifted into a one-ship landing zone atop Hill 823, nearly a mile to the south. Bombs from repeated air strikes had exploded on the crest all morning to blast out the tight LZ. Captain George Baldridge commanded Company B. He disposed his company in a defensive perimeter around the crest and sent a two-man observation post down the easy west slope, where enemy approach was most likely.

The two men were killed within ten minutes of setting up, by an enemy platoon attacking up the slope. It was the first of a series of assaults that afternoon which Company B held off with its own firepower. At times the enemy closed to within a few meters of the defense line before they were repulsed. Company B held firm, although the enemy harassed it with grenades as the light faded.

Company A under Captain James J. Muldoon had been slogging toward Company D's position. They reached its perimeter at about 1700 hours. Captain Muldoon's platoons were tired from the hard march. But they were fresher than the men of Company D, who had been fighting hard for three hours at close range. Company A filled the gaps in the perimeter.

The wounded could not be evacuated, nor could resupply be made. The NVA further up the slope poured heavy automatic weapons fire on the perimeter and against evacuation helicopters attempting to land. All night the North Vietnamese peppered the position with grenades, automatic weapons, and mortars.

Company C, meanwhile, had run into another enemy force. The time lost in overcoming it meant the company had to go into a night defensive position without linking up with Companies D and A.

Direct enemy pressure on Company B eased in late afternoon, but mortar rounds continued to drop on it. One of them wounded Captain Baldridge. Colonel Johnson swooped in with his command helicopter, dropping off his executive officer, Major Richard M. Scott and others to set up a forward battalion command post and evacuate a few of the more seriously wounded men. He also brought in Captain Ronald R. Leonard to assume command of Company B.

Major Scott, Captain Leonard, and others tightened the perimeter and reorganized it for defense just

Heavy fire from the enemy's 120mm mortars prevented dust-off helicopters from landing to evacuate US wounded. Based on a Soviet design, these heavy mortars had a maximum range of just over four miles. Operated by a five-man crew, they were broken down into three loads and pack-transported over the hills from Laos.

Dak To and Hill 875

TOUGH GOING:
Seven days after the savage fighting on Hill 823, US intelligence located a 2,000-strong enemy force further west at Hill 875. Here men of 2/503 work their way round a bomb crater at the base of the hill. The battalion's two companies advanced in eight columns up the hillside before encountering enemy fire.

before dusk. Just in time, because the enemy began probing again. One M79 gunner poked his head above the rim of a bomb crater when he heard noise in the bamboo. He blew off the head of an advancing NVA soldier only five meters away.

Through the night, enemy individuals and squads probed Company B's position, throwing grenades and firing rounds into it. The NVA made a heavier assault at 0330 but were repulsed at the perimeter.

Throughout the cold night, Air Force AC-47 'Shadow' gunships kept up a steady fire on nearby enemy positions. The AC-47s also dropped flares at

regular intervals, helping the men to spot enemy movement, and more important, to know that help was at hand.

On the morning of November 7, the enemy again attacked Company B. The paratroopers repulsed them with the help of air strikes, helicopter gun-ships, and the ever-present artillery. Company C joined up that morning with Companies A and D. Later in the day General Schweiter began sending in 1st Battalion, 503d Infantry to relieve the 4th Battalion. The relief was complete on November 8, and Colonel Johnson's battalion was withdrawn for a short rest. In the hard actions fought on November 6 - 7, it had damaged the NVA 66th Regiment badly and reduced the threat to Dak To.

The threat did not go away, however. Nor did 4/503 get to rest for long.

Besides the forces named earlier, intelligence analysts now believed the 174th NVA Regiment was also in the area. By November 15, its location was confirmed. It was in the vicinity of Hill 875, west of Dak To, with a strength of 2,000 men. Its mission was believed to be to cover the withdrawal of the 32d and 66th regiments west towards the Cambodian and Laotian borders.

Hill 875 is about five kilometers east of the Cambodian border, and about 12 kilometers southeast of the point where the borders of Laos, Cambodia, and Vietnam intersect. Its geographic coordinates are 14°34'N, 107°35'E.

On November 18, a Vietnamese 'Mike Force' company led by US Special Forces made contact with a force of NVA soldiers on the hill's east slope. After calling in Air Force and Marine air strikes the Mike Force withdrew back into the valley south of the hill. The enemy on Hill 875 was estimated to be in company strength.

The mission of securing Hill 875 was given to 2/503 on November 19. It planned to attack up the north slope of the hill with two rifle companies abreast and one in reserve. The Vietnamese Mike Force company would block the enemy line of retreat to the south of the hill.

The weather on November 19 was clear and warm. The ridge line leading to the top of Hill 875 was gradual and about 100 meters wide. It was thick with vegetation; mixed bamboo, scrub brush, and tall trees.

Companies C and D waited until artillery and air strikes had pounded the top of the hill before moving up the slope. Company D was on the left, C on the right. A trail that ran up the ridge line was the boundary between the companies. They moved with two platoons forward and one in reserve. Each platoon split into two columns. This made eight columns snaking up the hill through the thick brush and bamboo. The climb was a tense, plodding struggle through tangled vegetation made more tangled by the artillery and bomb strikes. The platoons

Flushing out a sniper —a trooper returns fire during operations. A quick response with as much firepower as possible rather than waiting for a chance of an accurate shot was recognized as the most effective tactic on first contact with the enemy.

Dak To and Hill 875

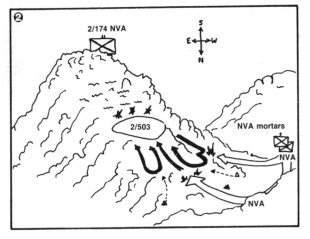

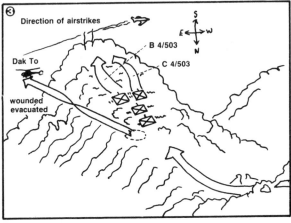

THE MOUSETRAP:
❶ Moment of contact on Hill 875 at about 1030 hrs. on November 19 as D and C companies, 2/503 run into concealed NVA defenses, while A Company is stretched thin defending flanks and rear. ❷ Four hours later the trap is sprung. While one NVA battalion holds off a two-company assault, another almost overwhelms A Company. Americans are outnumbered seven to one. ❸ Twenty-four hours later reinforcements from 4/503 reach the beleaguered 2d battalion. Three days later the hill was finally captured.

97

picked their best scouts to take the point, men they said could smell the NVA. They wanted all the warning they could get of the inevitable meeting with the enemy.

While Companies C and D moved slowly up the hill A Company remained anchored at the bottom in reserve while stretching out its own platoons to maintain contact with the other two companies. Its job: to provide flank and rear security, and to prepare a helicopter landing zone.

The scouts in front of Company D reached a slightly open area covered with fallen logs. The time was 10:30. One of the scouts whispered to his buddy, "I smell Charlies."

Small arms fire from a concealed position killed Specialist Fourth Class Kenneth Jacobson, the point man of 2d Squad, 2d Platoon, Company D. Immediately the troops of Company D dropped their rucksacks and began closing up, deploying in an assault line and heading toward the fight. The platoon medic came forward and was killed instantly. The concealed NVA troops began throwing grenades, giving away their position.

Company C on the right moved forward as well, dropping their rucksacks and swinging into a firing

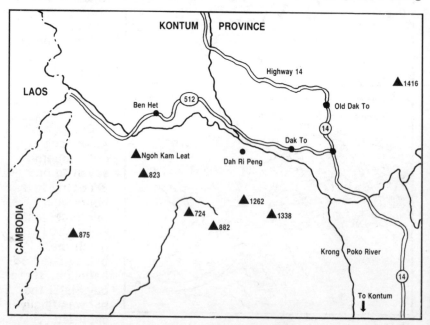

line. The men chanted and stomped their feet as they fired, yelling encouragement to one another.

The enemy fire increased. They were using AK-47s on full automatic, grenades, recoilless rifles, heavy mortars, and B-40 rockets.

The attackers popped smoke grenades to mark their position. Forward air controllers overhead and artillery forward observers on the ground called in friendly air strikes and artillery. But during the next four hours, in the heat of midday, and toiling up the steep slope, they were only able to push a short way up the hill, about 50 meters.

The assault bogged down in the tangle of underbrush and in face of the heavy fire from concealed positions. Companies C and D dug in as fast as they could rather than withdraw, so they could hold the ground gained so far. The front of the perimeter was only 20 meters from the NVA bunker where the battle started.

The noise was a crescendo of AK-47s stuttering, M-16s snapping, M-60 machine gun bursts adding their staccato, men screaming and yelling, all accompanied by the crump-crump-crump of artillery and rockets bursting. The steel and lead were invisible until they chewed into flesh or wood.

The medics were most vulnerable. Unarmed and carrying their aid kits, they had to expose themselves to minister to the casualties.

While the fight up the hill was developing, Captain Michael J. Kiley's Company A was stretched in a U-shape with its opening uphill. Its 2d and 3d platoons secured the flanks of Companies C and D, while the command group, weapons platoon, and 1st Platoon secured the rear.

When the fight began Captain Kiley ordered his weapons platoon to begin constructing a landing zone for helicopters to bring in supplies and evacuate casualties. They did so, swinging axes and machetes. The attached team of engineers from 173d Engineer Company began preparing demolition charges to blow the biggest trees.

Preparation of the LZ was slow and hard. At 1430, a helicopter dropped in an 'LZ Kit' of chain saws, cross saws, and axes to speed up the work. No one had to urge haste. The pointblank battle raged only 100 meters above. All the rucksacks were down on the damp ground now, and sweat poured off the

The Russian-designed AK-47 with its curved ammo magazine was the standard weapon for NVA infantry-men who were better equipped than their VC counterparts. The 7.62mm automatic rifle is effective up to 400 meters and can deliver 30 rounds from one magazine.

Dak To and Hill 875

PERIMETER WATCH: When the attack on Hill 875 ran into heavy fire from concealed enemy positions, the 173d went to ground to defend their gains. At some points their positions were only 20 meters from North Vietnamese bunkers. As automatic fire and artillery shredded the surrounding jungle the first priority was to take cover. Here a trooper sets up an M-60 machinegun position behind a log.

men, whether they were fighting or cutting down trees. Ammunition was being shot prodigiously. Resupply would be needed—soon.

Right after the LZ kit hit the ground, the NVA launched an attack against the rear and right flank

of Company A. The two attacking companies had
worked down the steep western slope of Hill 875 via
a series of prepared trails, which included steps cut
out of the mountainside with banisters attached for
handholds. Company A's rear observation post (OP)

PFC Carlos Lozada —awarded the Medal of Honor posthumously for providing covering fire for his squad as they retreated from an NVA advance.

at the foot of the hill saw the enemy first. The four-man group (three M-16 rifles and an M-60 machine gun) was led by Specialist Fourth Class James Kelly, squad leader. His machine gunner was Private First Class Carlos Lozada. Also in the team were Specialist Fourth Class John Steer and Private First Class Anthony Romano.

The team was split, with two men concealed behind trees or logs on both sides of the trail. Kelly began to hear twigs breaking in front of him. As he did, firing broke out to their left. Lozada yelled, "Here they come, Kelly," and began to fire his machine gun in long sweeping bursts down the trail into a group of 15 advancing NVA infantry. His first burst caught the NVA by surprise at the close range of ten meters, tearing up the column. But more NVA were advancing.

. At the same time, other OPs were being hit. Their firing alerted the rest of Company A. Men rushed forward from the perimeter to help Kelly's OP, but were hit by heavy enemy fire. Lozada shifted position, knelt behind a log, and kept firing long bursts into the advancing NVA. Kelly and Steer fired their M-16s from the other side of the trail.

They got the word to fall back. Lozada responded by running across the trail firing, and getting into position behind another log. From there he continued to spray the advancing NVA with a steady stream of machine gun fire. Kelly shot an NVA soldier at ten meters' range, then his M-16 jammed. While Kelly worked on his rifle, Lozada jumped into the trail. He began firing his machine gun from the hip at the oncoming NVA while walking slowly backward, covering Kelly and delaying the attackers.

Steer started dropping back. Kelly cleared his jammed weapon and started firing again. Then Lozada's M-60 jammed, and the NVA fire hit him in the head. He fell across Steer's legs. Kelly bent down and turned Lozada over so the NVA would see he was dead and wouldn't mutilate him. Kelly and Steer continued to withdraw, throwing M-26 fragmentation grenades at the NVA as they did.

The 2d and 3d Platoons of Company A had been up the slope evacuating wounded from Companies C and D. When the attack hit Kelly's and the other OPs, Captain Kiley, commanding Company A, ordered the 2d and 3d platoons on the radio to move down the hill to reinforce the 1st Platoon. It was his last transmission. Dozens of enemy mortar rounds burst on the LZ, wiping out Kiley's command group and further wounding the casualties lying there.

The 2d Platoon, on the west side of the ridge line, started back toward the LZ. They did not make it. An NVA attack hit their flank and front, cutting them off from the LZ and the rest of Company A. The platoon leader was hit in both arms and both legs, the platoon sergeant was wounded. Squad leaders were wounded or killed. The men of 2d Platoon consolidated as best they could and pulled back up the hill into the perimeter there.

The 3d Platoon, also under attack on the east of the ridge, suffered several casualties, but was able to make it to the LZ.

The NVA attacks were clearly closely coordinated, hitting both flanks and rear of Company A nearly simultaneously, supported by mortar and B-40 rocket fire. Each attack was made by an estimated company, far stronger than the understrength paratrooper platoons they smashed into. Many of the NVA were camouflaged.

Back at the LZ, Company A's wounded and few

DIGGING IN: There was no such thing as a spare minute on Hill 875. Every time there was a lull in the firing, the only thing to do was to dig in. The paratroops dug in with anything that came to hand — even helmets and knives. Here a Sky Trooper hurriedly excavates a foxhole. These shallow trenches, sometimes no more than two or three feet deep, could provide crucial cover against the enemy's remorseless mortar attacks.

remaining unwounded men began dragging up the hill to the C/D companies' perimeter, firing into what seemed like swarms of NVA troops. The weapons platoon had one good radio left, and took it along. The NVA cut the main trail for a brief time, but Companies C and D reopened it so that the survivors of Company A could be pulled inside.

The survivors of Company A had only their web gear (pistol belts with canteens, ammunition, and first aid dressing), helmets, and rifles. Their

Dak To and Hill 875

DIVE FOR COVER:
Going places on Hill 875 was a case of dashing from fallen tree trunk to fallen tree trunk to shell crater. There was plenty of cover, but the heavy undergrowth tangled by hours of shellfire and bomb blasts made sustained movement impossible. And sniper fire made standing up a dangerous activity almost anywhere on the hill.

rucksacks lay abandoned at the LZ. They had disassembled their 60mm mortar and brought it along. It was immediately put into action with Company D's mortars.

Company A's fighting had occupied only 30 minutes. The NVA followed its remnants right up to the perimeter, pressing the attack until halted by the fire from Companies C and D. At 1500, Company C reported to battalion HQ that about 200 - 300 NVA soldiers were all around them. Here is how the units

Dak To and Hill 875

CLEARING THE LZ: Troopers huddle behind a tree trunk as NVA automatic fire sweeps the LZ under construction on Hill 875. The enemy identified the LZ as critical to the reinforcement and re-supply strategy of the Sky Soldiers and fought ruthlessly to stop its creation. At one point possession of the LZ was split 50/50 between 2/503 and the NVA. The thickness of the sawn tree trunks shows the problems the US forces faced in creating the clearing.

were situated. Imagine looking up Hill 875 with the summit as 12 o'clock on a watch face. The units in the perimeter were disposed this way: Company D had from 7 to 12 o'clock, Company C from 12 around to 7 o'clock, and Company A's men intermingled

from 4 to 7 o'clock. The company command posts
were consolidated near the center, where the wounded were also collected and tended. Ammunition was
collected from the wounded and distributed to men
on the perimeter. In lulls in the firing, everyone kept

digging in. The NVA continued to press the attack on all sides, but were beaten off by the paratroopers. Ammunition was running low, however, and resupply was essential.

At 1550 hours, a helicopter from the 335th Assault Helicopter Company (radio call sign 'Cowboys') dropped in a load of ammunition. The ammo rolled down the hill outside the perimeter. It came to a stop about 15 meters in front, midway between the paratroopers and NVA. Two lieutenants organized a recovery party and moved out to retrieve the ammo. Most of it was hauled inside the perimeter, but enemy fire killed 1st Lieutenant Peter Lantz and forced the party to pull back.

The Cowboys kept trying to press through the heavy fire with resupply. The NVA had climbed into the tall trees above the perimeter. In the resupply effort, six helicopters were damaged and forced down. Heavy tactical air strikes and artillery were laid on the NVA positions while the resupply was attempted. The aircraft were A-1E Skyraiders and F-100 Super Sabres. They flew their passes on a path

WEAPONS OF THE SKY SOLDIERS: On Hill 875 a company's standard armory would include M-60 machine guns, M-79 grenade launchers and M-16 rifles. The grenade launcher was effective up to 400 yards—further than the reach of a hand grenade. Grenadiers carried up to 200 of the 40mm grenades in special pouch-lined jackets. In addition to the breech-loaded launcher every grenadier carried a revolver.

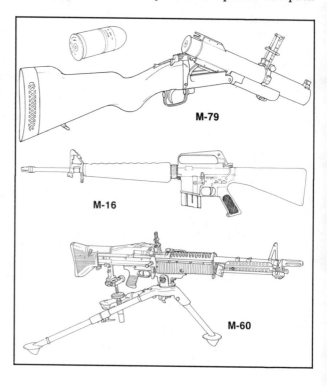

M-79

M-16

M-60

from southeast to northwest, at a tangent to the perimeter. Two hours after the resupply started, two pallets of mixed ammunition were successfully dropped into the perimeter at 1750, just before dark.

At dusk a jet fighter on a bomb pass flew in a different direction from the earlier passes. He came over the hill from northeast to southwest right over the perimeter. One of his bombs fell short. It burst in the middle of the Company C command post where the leaders and wounded were congregated. The errant bomb killed 42 and wounded 45 Sky Soldiers.

With so many leaders killed and wounded, the situation could have turned into confusion and panic. But leaders emerged from the ranks and discipline and control were maintained. The close bonds of training and shared combat held. Lieutenant Bartholomew O'Leary commanded Company D. Although seriously wounded, he remained in control throughout the night, maintaining communication with battalion and with the units in the perimeter. In Company C, Platoon Sergeant Peter Krawtzow took charge. Company A's Lieutenant Joseph Sheridan led his men, even though wounded.

Many of the battalion's radios were smashed or lost. The few remaining were essential for calling in artillery and air strikes. The artillery was directed to fire close to the perimeter, and kept bursting close around it throughout the night.

All the water and food in Company A was collected for the wounded. So were any blankets and clothing, to keep the wounded warm and to ward off shock. All night the paratroopers huddled between each other's legs in their holes in an attempt to keep warm. The temperature dropped into the low 50s; close to the dank ground the cold seeped into the bones. No one really slept.

Throughout the night the NVA kept probing, firing and moving in front of the position. The paratroopers threw grenades at the sounds, but did not fire their weapons. The muzzle flashes would have revealed their locations.

There was no resupply after dark. The little bit of food and water was kept for the wounded men. Most of the paratroopers went hungry and thirsty.

When the extent of the enemy on Hill 875 was realized, reinforcements were brought up. From the

Chaplain Charles J. Watters —a legendary figure who went into the field with leading units. The Catholic priest was awarded a posthumous Medal of Honor for his heroism on Hill 875. Unarmed and exposed, he ran through enemy fire to rescue fallen men who had been left outside the perimeter. Troopers tried to hold him back but the pastor shook them off. Three times he left the safety of the perimeter to rescue men until he himself was mortally wounded.

Dak To and Hill 875

HEAT OF THE BATTLE:

The height of the action on Hill 875 was a confusion of constant fire from weapons of all sizes from all sides, yelled appeals for artillery and air support on the RT, and muscle-straining dashes from one piece of shell-scarred cover to the next. As bullets and shrapnel smashed through the trees, it took guts to be on your feet and running.

The relief of Hill 875 — the map shows the disposition of US forces on November 20, 1967. The relief of 2/503 was hazardous and slow. To avoid ambush the three-company relief force of 4/503 marched off trail. The six-kilometer hike took all the hours of daylight before the first LZ at the base of 875 was reached.

4th Infantry Division, two companies of the 1st Battalion, 12th Infantry were flown in Air Force C-130s into the airstrip at Dak To. The battalion task force arrived after dark on the 19th, with the C-130s landing on a runway outlined by fire barrels burning a mixture of diesel and gasoline. It was immediately lifted by helicopters to the 173d's fire support base and placed under General Schweiter's command. Its mission: to conduct a supporting attack on Hill 875.

On the 20th, the morning mists cleared off quickly. The daylight brought fresh NVA probes with small arms and grenades. The priority of work for 2/503 on that morning was to hold the position and cut an LZ for resupply and evacuation of the wounded. The work went slowly. The men were exhausted and the trees large. A helicopter trying to drop an LZ kit was hit by fire from the high trees. Air strikes and artillery were run almost continuously while work on the LZ went forward with axes and machetes and the little bit of plastic explosive that remained.

The spot chosen for the LZ was on the right side of the battalion perimeter. The NVA pressed to within a few meters of it, and put men up into the trees to stop the work. One paratrooper said, "We secured half the LZ and the NVA the other half." Although helicopters tried all morning to evacuate wounded, none could get in. NVA rocket and mortar fire pounded the perimeter, while friendly artillery and air strikes pounded the NVA.

In midafternoon, Company D sent out a clearing patrol to kill some of the tree snipers. A captured M-60 machine gun firing from a concealed bunker cut down the first four men, pinning the patrol inside the perimeter.

During the day, the battalion attempted to drop in a command group to take over, but it could not get into the position.

Meanwhile, the 4th Battalion, 503d Infantry was coming to the relief of the perimeter, and 1/12 Infantry was moving from Dak To and consolidating at the 173d's forward fire support base.

The paratroopers of 4/503 were eager to go to the relief of their comrades of their sister 2d Battalion. Lieutenant Colonel James H. Johnson commanded 4/503, nicknamed the 'Geronimo' battalion. He briefed his company commanders on the situation and the mission. He warned them of the enemy strength on Hill 875, and the possibility of ambush along the relief route.

The battalion was lifted to a fire base within six kilometers of Hill 875 in late afternoon of the 19th. It was too late to move forward more than three miles through the jungle at night. The men cleaned their weapons and stocked up on extra ammunition in preparation for a hard day's fighting. They carried less food than usual to maximize their ammo load.

In the dawn light of November 20, Company B, 4/503 swung out on the relief march, followed by Companies A and C. Captain Ronald R. Leonard, Company B's commander, heeded the warning that his force might be ambushed en route. He decided to approach Hill 875 off trails. The company moved in a diamond formation, navigating through the scrub and bamboo on compass azimuths. Along the way, they crossed several trails and found NVA base camps. The camps were littered with NVA bodies and pieces of bodies blown apart by artillery and air strikes.

Their navigation brought Company B, 4/503, into the right spot at 1600 hours. They were on the ridge leading through Company A2/503's old position and onward up Hill 875. They filled their canteens from the stream at the base of the hill.

Bringing ammo the hard way —troopers of 4/503 hump ammo boxes up Hill 875 in preparation for the final assault.

Moving forward, they found a dead young paratrooper surrounded by a mound of empty shell casings, still clutching his M-60 machine gun. They also found 15-20 full magazines of 5.56mm ammunition for M-16 rifles which Company A had dropped. Co.B4/503 pushed on up the hill towards the 2d Battalion. En route they passed dead paratroopers, bloody Chinese first aid dressings, NVA and US rucksacks, and empty Chinese ammunition cans.

Darkness was coming on. Guidance from Colonel Johnson in a command and control helicopter and signalling rounds from 2/503 pointed the way.

Company B's lead platoon reached the 2d Battalion's perimeter first. The men from 2/503 greeted the fresh troopers with tears and hugs. The rest of Company B closed in quickly. They passed out their water and rations, and put their medics to work with the wounded from 2/503. Companies A and C of 4/503 were right behind, moving rapidly through the

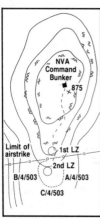

November 22, 1967 —The beleaguered troopers of 2/503 have been relieved and the three companies of 4/503 have secured the perimeter of the second LZ at the base of the hill.

gathering darkness. All were inside the perimeter between 2100 and 2200.

Before the light faded, Major William Kelly, the executive officer of 2d Battalion, jumped into the perimeter. He took control of the forces in the strengthened position. The ship Kelly jumped from was the only helicopter able to get into the perimeter before dark. It took out five of the most critically wounded men.

The men settled in for another cold night. Most were still short on food and water.

The night of the 20th remained quiet. The paratroopers continued to dig in, making overhead cover from anything available. Again, they huddled together to keep off the dank chill. The men kept on 50 percent alert, half of them awake and half trying to sleep. Those awake watched the moon rise above the trees. It rose soon after midnight, but they could not see it from the foxholes until much later. They waited for attacks that did not come, and spent time comforting the scores of wounded, and trying to keep warm.

On the 21st, 4/503 was to attack up Hill 875 at 1000 hours. But the attack was delayed for resupply of ammunition. Helicopters braved the usual fire to drop in LAWs (a 66mm light antitank weapon for use against bunkers), flamethrowers, and two 81mm mortars with 400 rounds of ammunition. More 60mm mortar ammunition was also dropped in.

After delays for air strikes and artillery preparations, the attack started at 1505. The 4th Battalion pushed forward with its A and B companies abreast and C Company in reserve. They fought hard for two hours, taking more than 50 casualties, but could not pass a number of concealed and impregnable bunkers. The men had to crawl over logs and around trees, exposing themselves to snipers on the flanks and high in the trees. Also, they could not actually see the NVA firing from camouflaged six-inch slots from the bunkers. The flamethrowers were not much use as the men had not been trained to use them. Mortar fire was ineffective against the bunkers, since several feet of earth was piled over their log roofs.

Despite the heavy enemy fire, the men of Company A yelled, chanted, and cursed at the NVA as they attacked. Some sang paratrooper songs as they

Dak To
and
Hill 875

EVACUATION:
A wounded trooper is helped to safety by two of his buddies. No helicopter evacuation was possible until the fight to create a secure Landing Zone at the foot of Hill 875 had been won.

crawled and fired or threw grenades. After two
hours, the 4/503 had to halt the attack and withdraw
into the perimeter. At that time, two of Company
B's rifle platoons were down to strengths of 14 and
nine men. Meanwhile, during the day while the hill

Dak To and Hill 875

DUSTOFF:
From a tight landing zone hacked out of the hardwood trees a UH-1 Dustoff medevac helicopter evacuates a wounded trooper. Debris of the battle lies in the foreground. Prompt helicopter evacuation kept the death rate among the wounded below one in a hundred — which made the situation on Hill 875 even more alarming before the LZ could be created and defended.

was being pounded and attacked by 4/503, a new LZ was cut on the left side of the lower ridge. Although it was under constant enemy fire from nearby hills, the many wounded were evacuated.

The night of November 21 - 22 was very quiet by

comparison with the two before. During the day of
November 22, the troops remained in the perimeter.
They directed air strikes and artillery against the
enemy above them on Hill 875. Besides the 105mm
artillery of the 173d's own 3d Bn. 319th Artillery,
support came from heavier 155mm, 8-inch,
and 175mm artillery brought up for the purpose. The
NVA on 875 and nearby hills continued to drop mortar rounds and rockets into the perimeter.

On November 22, Major Long's 1/12 Infantry was
lifted into an LZ on the south slope of Hill 875. It
began moving up the south slope toward an assigned limit of advance, to be in position for a coordinated attack on the 23d. The 1/12 troops had also
loaded up with extra ammunition and had been
issued 25 LAWs for use against the bunkers.

The battalion moved slowly through the jungle,
sweating heavily under the weight of the ammunition in the humid 85-degree heat. The battalion
came across unoccupied NVA bunkers and smelled

Dak To and Hill 875

UNDER FIRE:
A squad takes cover from heavy enemy fire.
It was at moments like this that the M-79 came into its own. With the rest of the squad pinned down and unable to aim, a trooper equipped with a grenade launcher would carefully calculate the enemy's position and then fire the grenade on a lobbed trajectory without lifting his head above the parapet.

decaying flesh. While air strikes pounded the top of 875, the 1/12 reached its limit of advance in late afternoon and set up a perimeter for the night.

The morning of the 23d found the NVA troops still in heavy fortifications atop Hill 875. But the paratroopers and 1/12 Infantry were ready to assault. Word was passed by radio in code for a coordinated attack to begin at 1100. Again artillery and air strikes would precede the attack, firing all morning. Satchel charges, tear gas grenades, and 90mm recoilless rifles were dropped in for use against the enemy bunkers.

The plan called for 4/503 to attack up the north slope and 1/12 up the south slope. In the 4/503, Company B would move on the left and Company C on the right, with Company A in reserve, favoring reinforcement of Company B.

Company D of the 1/12 Infantry would lead that attack, with Company A right behind them.

Before the attack, the NVA on 875 and nearby

Dak To and Hill 875

BUNKER PROTECTION: The cutaway shows how the NVA's well-prepared defenses were able to withstand USAF air strikes for so long. Crossed logs and thick earth cover overhead made them immune to anything less than a lucky direct hit from a 500 lb. bomb or 105mm shell. Detection was almost impossible as the bunkers had been built well before the events of November 1967 and the undergrowth had grown back, giving the enemy the advantage of full concealment.

hills dropped mortar rounds on the assembling forces, trying to disrupt the attack. (The 1st and 3d battalions of the NVA's 174th Regiment were just west of Hill 875. It was 1st Battalion that had mauled Company A, 2/503, at the base of Hill 875.)

The artillery and air kept smashing the top of the hill as the attacking troops moved forward. The companies kept their own mortars firing in support. They put the bursts 25 meters in front of the lead troops and walked them forward slowly. By this

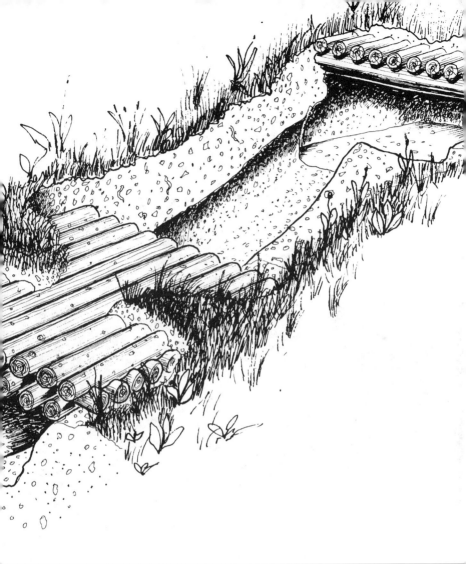

time, the NVA 2d Battalion, 174th Regiment, on top of the hill was about gone. Its few survivors kept up the fight, but resistance dwindled as the paratroopers and 1/12 Infantry closed the ring around the summit.

The paratroopers of 4/503 reached the summit of Hill 875 at 1122 hours on Thanksgiving Day. Three minutes later, men of Company D, 1/12 Infantry linked up with them.

The troopers raised cheers of "Airborne" and

Victory in sight —elation and relief begin to show on the face of this sergeant of 4/503 and RTO as they summon artillery support during the final attack.

"Geronimo," then cried with happiness, pride and relief that they had made it.

The top of Hill 875 was blown bald and dusty by the incessant air and artillery strikes. But concealed fortifications still stood firm and undamaged,

Dak To and Hill 875

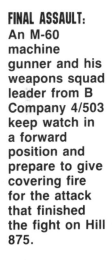

FINAL ASSAULT:
An M-60 machine gunner and his weapons squad leader from B Company 4/503 keep watch in a forward position and prepare to give covering fire for the attack that finished the fight on Hill 875.

testimony to their construction. In one bunker, the men found the date 3/7/67 carved in a log, testimony to the deliberate preparation of the position months before.

Evacuation of the wounded and dead paratroopers

began soon after Hill 875 was secure. Men sat in the dust and debris to open cans of C-ration meals and drink some water. Later on Thanksgiving Day insulated food containers with the traditional meal were flown in.

Hill 875 was turned over to 1/12 Infantry. They policed the battlefield for two days, then departed on November 26 for operations farther west, near the Cambodian/Laotian border. Hill 875 fell quiet.

The encounter on Hill 875 was not a casual meeting engagement between opposing forces moving about. Instead, it was a place where the NVA expected to fight, and to impose a heavy cost on the US attackers. Colonel Johnson and his men said that all NVA soldiers appeared in good health, were well turned out and excellently equipped. He said the readiness of the equipment was most impressive. Every item in the hundreds of captured NVA packs — sweaters, mosquito nets, rice rolls, and ammunition — was brand-new. Mortars and rocket launchers bore manufacture dates of 1967. It was evident, Johnson said, that the 174th Regiment had been completely equipped with new weapons and clothing before crossing into South Vietnam.

The NVA troops had prepared a complex defensive system on Hill 875 several months earlier. The natural growth had time to repair the scars of constructing the system of interconnecting trenches, bunkers, and tunnels. It was a formidable natural fortress, manned by fresh and full-strength units supported by similar ones in nearby mortar range.

Overhead cover of the NVA fighting positions was a combination of logs and dirt. Bunkers were flush with the ground. Most had short tunnels leading outward in the rear or from connecting trenches. Bunkers were sited for mutual support and interlocking fire, deadly against attackers.

The battalions of the 503d found that fragmentation grenades had little effect unless thrown squarely through the bunker apertures. Heavy napalm from flamethrowers was not effective unless poured into apertures and ignited by white phosphorus. White phosphorus grenades and 20-pound satchel charges of plastic explosive (which were not issued to the assault troops) were effective against the bunkers.

After the battle, the bodies of 719 NVA soldiers

The Medal of Honor —awarded posthumously to three members of the 173d for their heroism at Dak To. The three Dak To recipients were PFC John A Barnes III, PFC Carlos J. Lozada and Chaplain (Maj.) Charles J. Watters.

KING OF THE HILL: The most bitter battle of the war is over. Just below the summit of Hill 875 Major Richard Scott, executive officer of 4/503, surveys the area and sorts out what has to be done. In the background his men begin to explore the network of well-prepared enemy bunkers. Dates on NVA supplies and ammunition recovered showed that the fortifications had been prepared several months earlier, an indication that the actions at Dak To were not a chance encounter but a deliberate part of Hanoi's strategy.

were counted on Hill 875. Nine men of the 174th Regiment were taken prisoner.

Company A, 2/503, went into the battle on Hill 875 on November 19 with 101 officers and men. When it was finally extracted from Hill 875 on November 23, Company A mustered just one officer and 27 men.

The fight at Hill 875 and the other fierce battles along the border in October, November, and early December 1967 hurt the NVA forces badly. But Hanoi was willing to take the casualties. It had drawn US popular attention to the bloody battles, and had directed MACV's focus to the border areas. Behind those diversions, Hanoi moved ahead with preparations for the 1968 Tet offensive. That would hit in the cities, far from the bloody green hills, at the end of January 1968, two months hence.

Dak To was only a tiny speck on the situation maps in Saigon, Hanoi, and Washington. Hill 875 was dwarfed by the higher mountains around it. The undergrowth on Hill 875 repaired itself in a few months. But the blood and courage of the 173d's young paratroopers wrote Dak To and Hill 875 into the immortal register of gallant US military actions.

Pacify and Control

Keeping the Gains

AFTER President Nixon took office in January 1969, the missions of US units in Vietnam changed.

This time, their role was to be pacification: protecting the people in the countryside so that the South Vietnamese army could take a more active combat role. The 173d was assigned a tough area to pacify: coastal Binh Dinh province. That was one of the three it had been stretched thin to cover since early 1968. Now Binh Dinh would have the brigade's whole attention.

Binh Dinh lies south of Quang Ngai and north of Cam Ranh bay. Binh Dinh province was always a tough province for whoever tried to control Indochina from the 1930s onward. It had been under enemy control for years. The 3d North Vietnamese Army Division operated from mobile base camps in the mountains. Its three infantry regiments — the 2d, 18th, and 22d — had operated with impunity in the area for years. The 1st Air Cavalry Division had fought the NVA and VC in Binh Dinh through most of 1966, with heavy casualties on both sides.

Although repeated operations had been run through the province by the ARVN, Korean, and US forces, control of Binh Dinh was not in the hands of the South Vietnamese government. In fact, the population was very much still in the balance. Everyone since the Japanese had taken a shot at pacifying Binh Dinh. Now it was the 173d's turn.

The name for pacification of Binh Dinh was Washington Green: a bland title for a very difficult challenge. It began in mid-April 1969.

Brigadier General John W. Barnes commanded the 173d then. Talking about the different war the brigade was to pursue in pacification, he said, "It's no longer a big unit war. We've forced the enemy

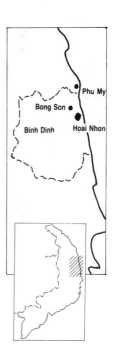

Brig. Gen. John W. Barnes —commanded the 173d at the start of the pacification era. He identified the Sky Soldiers role as securing hamlets and denying the VC grassroots support.

to fragment his forces to avoid detection. And in turn, we have done likewise and gone after him, saturating the areas he once could call his own, meeting him on his own terms, ferreting him out and destroying him. Of course, this has put a great responsibility on the small unit leader. It has become a squad and platoon leader's war."

Barnes emphasized to the troops that the brigade would no longer be preoccupied with chasing and killing enemy troops in unpopulated jungle and mountain areas. He said the brigade's mission would be to secure the people, their homes, and their farms,

Pacify and Control

CHANGE OF PACE:
A helmetless
paratrooper of
C Company,
4/503d watches
Vietnamese
militiamen as
they check a
peasant's
burden during
the rebuilding
of a hamlet in
northern Binh
Dinh province.
The hamlet had
been destroyed
in a Viet Cong
raid two years
earlier.
These secure-
and-pacify
operations
were a marked
change to the
pitched battles
of earlier years.

with the aim being to deny the VC their support from the hamlets.

Each maneuver battalion operated in a single district of the province. Each battalion set up an operations center at the district headquarters, along with local Vietnamese units.

The 1/503 operated in Hoai An district. 2/503 was in Hoai Nhon district, with its headquarters at Bong Son, the largest town in northern Binh Dinh. 4/503 went into Tam Quan district. The 1st Battalion, 50th Infantry, worked in Phu My. (It was put under operational control of the 173d while the 3/503 was temporarily taken from brigade control to operate under Task Force South, on the II - III corps border.)

The pacification plan was to begin security operations in 24 hamlets. As a hamlet and its surrounding area were deemed pacified, the 173d's forces could withdraw gradually and perform the same mission at other hamlets.

Thus the battalions broke down the districts into company-sized chunks, and the companies and platoons did the same. The method was to locate Sky Soldiers right with Vietnamese units in the villages. The Vietnamese in this case were Regional Force (RF) and Popular Force (PF), a sort of home guard militia or national guard in US terms. Their nickname was 'Ruff-Puffs,' from the usual linking of their acronyms as RF/PF.

Emphasis in Washington Green was on training the Ruff-Puffs to develop them into a semblance of trained soldiers. Eventually the Americans would be withdrawn. The Vietnamese regular forces and the Ruff-Puffs would then provide security for the people and keep the Viet Cong and NVA away.

Breaking up the 173d's battalions, companies, and platoons and dispersing them among the villages created a visible American security presence in the eyes of the people. It also made the job of training the Ruff-Puffs simpler, because they and the Americans were side by side. However, the dispersion created severe control problems. Assembling a rifle company could take hours, for instance.

Also, the rules for firing weapons ('rules of engagement') were very restrictive. This was in line with the nature of the pacification mission. The reasoning was that you do not pacify villagers by pounding their homes with artillery and air strikes. All free-fire zones were abolished. The rules on artillery forbade use of high explosive rounds within 1,000 meters of inhabited areas. This virtually eliminated its use in the densely populated coastal lowlands.

For the troopers of the 173d, the pacification mission was a sharp departure from the brigade's earlier battles in War Zones C and D, in Junction City, and at Dak To. In those engagements the enemy was in force, the fight concentrated on him, and the full weight of artillery and air could be concentrated to kill him.

Now, however, the enemy was elusive. The North

SP4 Michael R. Blanchfield —awarded a posthumous Medal of Honor for his gallantry during a hamlet search in Binh Dinh province. When a suspect ran from a hut and threw a grenade, the 19-year-old trooper fell on it to absorb the blast, saving the lives of four of his colleagues and several civilians.

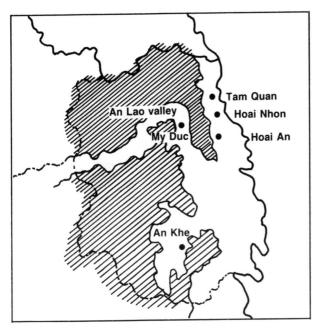

PACIFICATION ZONE:
Binh Dinh
province, which
included the
important
provincial
capital of An
Khe, was
critical to the
enemy's plans.
By winning
control of it
and the
neighboring
province to the
west, the NVA
could claim to
have cut South
Vietnam in two.
But occupying
it stretched
NVA forces and
the task of
retaining the
inhabitants'
loyalty was left
to VC units.
The US
countered by
dispatching
the 173d to
begin
Operation
Washington
Green. The 20-
month program
involved
educating local
military cadres,
restoring the
fishing industry
at Tam Quan,
and defending
the area.

Vietnamese regiments that had imposed their own 'pacification' on Binh Dinh had been moved elsewhere by the high command in Hanoi. The NVA had turned over the province to the Viet Cong units they had trained and controlled. The VC units in the area stayed in the nearby mountains during the day. When directed, they moved back into the populated areas at night for recruiting and resupply, and to keep the people aware that they were still around.

Most families had members in the guerrilla forces. They also had family members or relations in the RF and PF units. People in the area had been fighting occupiers and coexisting with guerrillas for nearly three decades. The 173d was the newest occupying force, and could expect to get about the same reception from the population as its predecessors.

The Viet Cong and their sympathizers in the villages sowed the district with booby traps of all types, ranging up to 155mm artillery rounds rigged to explode when tripped. Booby traps are especially nasty weapons, if degrees of nastiness are thinkable. You trip one, and you do not know if you will lose a toe, a leg, or be blown to bits. Since they were concealed and meant to surprise, combatting them required the highest order of vigilance. The mission

Pacify and Control

HOOTCH SEARCH: However routine the operation, or apparently friendly the villagers, hut-to-hut searches were always tense situations. As the war progressed Viet Cong booby traps became increasingly ingenious and effective. A survey showed booby traps responsible for one in ten US fatalities and 15 percent of wounds among US soldiers serving in Vietnam from 1965 - 1970.

had a high frustration level. The normal reaction of the 173d's troopers was to fix and close with the enemy. But with booby traps, there was no enemy to fix. Or he might even be one of the civilians standing in the shade watching the medevac helicopter whop-whopping in to take out young men who had been horribly mangled by a booby trap, but still had a chance at life if lifted to a hospital immediately.

All of this change required a high level of discipline and diplomacy down to the individual

trooper. It required a difficult mental shift. But the
men adapted. As 1st Lieutenant James F. O'Brien,
of the 1/503, said: "The pacification effort called for
the proverbial patience of the Orient, as well as their
own Western aggressiveness." But he showed the
difficulty of the brigade's task when he said of the
people in his district: "The one element of relative
stability and security was the Viet Cong, with pro-
mises of land for all and dreams of a better life.
Husbands, sons, and fathers willingly invested their

lives in expectation of the day when they could stand free, as no man's peasant."

A major part of the pacification effort involved law and order. The 173d Military Police detachment worked with the engineers and cavalry to control

Pacify and Control

CAPTURED SUPPLIES: Officers (left) inspect Soviet-made 122mm rocket rounds still in the bamboo backpacks that the enemy used to transport them over the mountains. Men of 2/503 (far left) heft rice bags from a cache near Bong Son. Finding enemy supplies was almost an accidental event during early operations in Vietnam. Under pacification it was an important part of cutting the enemy from his support in the field.

traffic and escort convoys on the roads and in the villages. In 1969, the MPs received the new Commando V-100 wheeled armored escort vehicle. They emblazoned the V-100s with brigade patches, parachute wings, and 'Military Police' signs, creating a visible law enforcement presence along the roads. In addition, the MPs set up a combined law enforcement operations center with the Vietnamese National Police and the ARVN military police in the province.

The brigade's security of the roads and outside the villages released the Vietnamese RF/PFs to defend the hamlets. To accomplish that, the 173d's squads and platoons became teachers. They trained the RF/PF in basic military crafts: keeping their weapons clean, marksmanship, security, and the rest.

Two examples show how the pacification program worked. The first involved the fishing industry in Tam Quan. Since 1966, the Saigon government had restricted fishing to control VC infiltration through the waters of Tam Quan inlet. Fish production dropped. The local market went stagnant, since so few fish were available. Only a few diehard fishermen plied the waters when government patrols were out of sight.

A platoon of 4/503 moved in and set up security with local RF forces on April 20. They arranged a system of escorting fishing boats into the richer waters outside the three-kilometer restricted zone. The brigade's boat and hamlet officials stayed out with the fleet and escorted them back in late afternoon with their catch. The catch was sold in Tam Quan marketplace. Seeing the results there, two neighboring hamlets asked to be included in the escort arrangement so their fishermen could do the same. Gradually the government restrictions were lifted and escort reduced until only a night curfew remained. In less than three months, Thien Chanh hamlet had more than 2,000 residents and the Tam Quan market was thriving.

My Duc hamlet was different. Well inland at the mouth of the An Lao valley, it had been deserted by its former residents. They squatted in refugee camps in Bong Son. The fields lay fallow.

Troops of 2/503 moved into My Duc along with an RF security element. No one lived there. The troops were alone for a while. The brigade's 173d Engineer Company rebuilt the bridge the VC had destroyed. The road was secured, and resupply for the troops came over it by truck so that people could see that the security forces intended to remain. Gradually people began drifting back, bringing their cattle to

Staff Sgt. Laszlo Rabel —was on long-range patrol in the hills of Binh Dinh when his surveillance team detected enemy movement. Suddenly a grenade landed in their midst. Sgt. Rabel threw himself on it, sacrificing his own life to save his men. He was awarded the Medal of Honor.

graze and to work the fallow rice fields. Then they began building houses among the ruins. Again in less than three months, people settled in. More than 160 families were living in the rebuilt My Duc hamlet by midsummer.

Although the Viet Cong tried to turn the people against the Americans, they were not always successful. The story is told of an eight-year-old boy named Khan. Khan lived in a hamlet on the Bong Son coast. He made friends with the Sky Soldiers when they moved into his hamlet. In that area, the VC told the people they would 'take steps' against persons who fraternized with the Americans. Khan continued to associate with the troopers. The VC killed his father.

Still he visited his Sky Soldier friends. For that, the VC came one night and cut off the boy's left arm. The Americans saved his life and got medical care for him in the field. In time, Khan's stump healed. As it did, he resumed visiting his GI friends. The Viet Cong came again and killed his mother.

After his mother's death, Khan moved in with his uncle. The VC finally left him alone. He visited the Sky Soldiers every day. He was a source of inspiration and cheer for them. One of his favorite tasks was filling their canteens with fresh water from the hamlet well.

The well was a cylindrical deep hole, with a built-up rim. The women would lean on the rim and drop their buckets into the well on ropes. Khan, however, with his single arm and agile feet, would climb down the well to fill a bucket and then bring it up to fill the canteens in turn.

According to men of the 173d, neither Khan's spirit nor his good cheer were clouded by his family tragedy. He remained friends with the Sky Soldiers until they finally left his hamlet. They wonder now what happened to him after they departed.

The tempo of enemy activity accelerated in November and December 1969. The 22d NVA Regiment moved into the An Lao Valley. That threatened to disrupt pacification in two districts of the province.

On November 3, NVA sappers hit fire support bases Stinger and Mahoney in near-simultaneous attacks just before dawn. The attacks were repulsed because the troopers had maintained an alert and

Brig. Gen. Hubert S. Cunningham —took command of the 173d in August 1969 just as the pacification operation was having effect. As a result the enemy changed tactics and began to leave its mountain retreat hideaways and make forays to disrupt pacification.

Pacify and Control

CAVALRY STYLE:
A jeep crew of E troop, 17 Cav swings into action while on road security for the 173d in Binh Dinh province. The squad leader (left) directs the fire of the .50-cal. machine gunner at the same time as calling in an artillery strike on the radio, while an assistant gunner prepares another ammo box.

active defense. The 3d Battalion, 319th Artillery, at Stinger vindicated again the 173d's policy of having the artillerymen provide their own defense. They bloodied the attackers at light cost to themselves. The same result occurred at Mahoney, held by the

Pacify and Control

MISSION IMPOSSIBLE: The more the war progressed, the more adept the Sky Troopers became at using their Hueys to land men where no LZ was available. Here a UH-1D demonstrates its ability to deliver troops onto a seemingly impossible ridge. Making the jump on to the steep slope are men of the 173d's 1/50 Mech Infantry during a quick-reaction mission near Bong Son.

4/503 Infantry. The next NVA reaction was to shell the brigade headquarters camp with mortar and recoilless rifle fire on the night of November 11. The attack inflicted little damage, but it reminded the troopers that the war had no 'rear' or front line

and that the NVA were back. The NVA next struck at a hamlet called An Qui. There, Company A, 4/503 Infantry, had established its command post along with the hamlet security forces. The attack came at 0330. Captain Richard Timmons, the company commander, had set up roving patrols. They detected the intruders and reacted aggressively. They killed ten and captured the lone survivor of an 11-man NVA raiding force. Over the Christmas and New Year of 1969 - 70 the intelligence picture showed that a regi-

ment of the 3d NVA Division had moved onto Hill 474, in the An Lao valley west of Tam Quan district. The hill was composed of huge boulders bigger than buildings that created thousands of caves and tunnels. It was best described as an upside-down bowl of popcorn.

At first, the troopers tried the conventional method of attack. That did not work; the enemy was too well protected in the caves from US artillery fire. Even 105mm high explosive rounds fired directly

WORKING TOGETHER: Men of 1/503, operating with Vietnamese troops, run to defensive positions during recon missions in the Nui Mum hills.

into the hill had little effect. The hill itself had no value. Taking it by infantry assault would mean nothing. So the brigade laid siege to the NVA regiment. With an infantry battalion attached from the 101st Airborne Division, and its own 3/503, plus artillery, it kept the hill encircled.

The hill was pounded day and night with artillery and air strikes. The 51st Chemical Detachment used CH-47 Chinook helicopters to pour thousands of gallons of thickened fuel on the hill. The fuel seeped down into the caves. Thermite grenades were dropped, igniting the fuel.

The 3/503, and the 3/506 from the 101st Airborne Division patrolled and set up ambushes at night to catch the NVA troops filtering out in small groups. Sometimes they would make contact, other times find evidence that some NVA soldiers had slipped through. Occasionally they would capture some.

Finally Hill 474 was quiet. A prisoner led the troops to the regimental commander's office deep inside the hill. Situation maps covered with clear acetate remained on the wall. The prisoner showed the troopers a ledge overlooking a pit. He told them that was where the NVA threw their dead. The stench wafting up from the pit agreed. A trooper was lowered over the ledge on a 100-foot nylon line to investigate. He reached the end of the line but did not touch bottom. He was hauled back up, and another 100-foot line added. He was lowered again to the extent of the line. Still no bottom. He dropped rocks, but could not hear them hit. He was hauled back up again. The pit was left undisturbed.

Also in January 1970, 1/503 in Hoai An district decided the RF and PF troops were ready to take on a larger role in security in the low country. That would release its units to operate back in the mountains. Disrupting the VC at the source would improve security of the lowlands.

The battalion returned to conducting 'Hawk' team operations perfected in late 1968. Small patrols of fire team size (five or six men) were lifted by helicopter into the mountains above the fertile plains being pacified.

These reconnaissance patrols stayed out for four days or so, hunting for the enemy. When the enemy was located, the Hawk teams assaulted him, maintaining contact until the enemy was destroyed or

Sign at Fire Support Base Kelly — it was one of several FSBs operated by 3rd BN, 319th Artillery in support of the 173d during pacification operations.

broke contact himself. The renewed success of the Hawk concept surprised even its advocates, according to officers of 1/503. The months of training the RF and PF forces in basic military skills paid off for the Sky Troopers. Through teaching the RF/PFs, the men were themselves sharper in the basic military skills.

Like the Hawk teams, the Rangers operated in small groups in the mountains. Hawk operations were conducted by the normal infantry units. Using the troops they had, the Hawk operations were an effective way of keeping the VC off balance. But the Rangers and their missions were different.

Company N, 75th Rangers, was the 'eyes and ears' of the brigade, human collectors of intelligence about the enemy. They operated far back in the mountains, 30 - 40 kilometers, well beyond supporting artillery range. The Ranger company was built up to a strength of 130 men about this time. With that strength, seven or eight teams of five men each could be in the bush at all times. Every hour, they fed information by radio into a Ranger operation center at the 173d tactical headquarters. For the brigade's intelligence officers, the Ranger information was an invaluable resource because it came from trained observers.

One of the 75th Rangers, Patrick Tadina, was legendary. He served in Vietnam for nearly five and one-half years. He landed with the 173d in May 1965, and served continuous tours until rotating to Hawaii in the autumn of 1970.

Staff Sergeant Patrick Tadina of Honolulu stood 5 feet 5 inches tall and weighed 130 pounds. He was a mainstay noncommissioned officer of Company N, 75th Rangers. By mid-1970, he had led more than 200 fellow Americans in combat patrols. Not one was killed, a tribute to his leadership and combat skills (and bountiful supply of good luck).

Sergeant Tadina always walked the point, first to make contact with the enemy. In the mountains, he carried a 60-pound rucksack and a communist assault rifle. The rifle, his floppy bush hat, and long hair always caused the NVA to hesitate when they saw him, or even to call out a greeting. Those split seconds of delay gave Sergeant Tadina the opportunity to shoot first and gain the advantage. It also gave his men the warning they needed to move into

Brig. Gen. Elmer R. Ochs —took command of the 173d for the last three months of the pacification campaign. He had been deputy commander of the 173d as a colonel when selected for promotion to brigadier general. His assumption of command assured continuity at the top.

Pacify and Control

HAWK TEAM:
An M-79 grenadier moving up a rocky stream on a deep penetration 'Hawk' patrol in the mountains of Binh Dinh. The Hawk teams of five or six men were heli-lifted into the mountains to locate and fight the enemy. The grenadier's 60 lb. backpack made hunting VC in rough terrain a job for only the fittest. Combined with the surveillance patrols in the lowlands, the Hawk teams were an important element in the 173d's strategy of denying the enemy any hiding place.

the assault ahead of enemy reactions. He was decorated 12 times for heroism (including two Silver Stars) and wounded three times.

No other Sky Troopers matched Sergeant Tadina's tenure, but by late 1970, many were men back in Vietnam on second and third tours.

One was Captain Joseph W. Moore, commander of Company B, 2d Battalion, 503d Infantry. He observed that if the individual US soldier went for as long as a month without making significant contact with the enemy, he tended to become complacent and relax. To reverse that tendency required continuous attention by small unit leaders.

A captured VC document gave the view from the other side. It said:

"US troops clumsy and vulnerable to boobytrapping and mining. US troops discard munitions and valuable equipment. (They) sleep on ambush."

Captain Moore stressed the need to keep troops in combat gear during pacification operations. Although enemy contact was less frequent and lighter than during the early years in War Zones C and D, men could be killed and wounded by even light contact. Training and discipline were the keys to preventing complacency in the difficult pacification mission.

Staff Sgt. Glenn H. English —in an M-113 armored personnel carrier when it was ambushed. Despite severe burns he rallied his men to rout the enemy. He died when his vehicle exploded as he tried to pull a wounded man inside to safety. He was posthumously awarded the Medal of Honor.

That meant weapons firing, day and night patrolling, hard work, and attention to watching for even the smallest indications of VC presence. To Captain Moore, pacification was harder than search-and-destroy because it demanded more intelligence and maturity from the troops.

At the same time they were dealing with the local populace, the troops had to be ready to fight and kill the enemy who was trying to kill them.

Another captured VC document provides the final verdict on the pacification operations by the 173d:

"Presence of US and RF troops in the hamlet areas are making it difficult to procure rice and supporters will not rally. Sympathizers are dwindling and popular support is low. The mountains are no longer a sanctuary . . . US troops choose to fight under all circumstances and will insanely pursue us into the mountains . . ."

The Sky Soldiers had proved they had flexibility and intelligence to match their raw courage in battle.

Winding Down

IN 1971, the drawdown of US ground combat units in Vietnam accelerated. Major fighting units had already left in 1969 and 1970 as the Nixon Administration 'Vietnamized' the war.

The 9th Infantry Division had arrived in 1966. It departed in late 1969, leaving one brigade in Vietnam. The 1st Infantry Division left in April 1970, going back to Fort Riley and Germany. The 9th Infantry Division's remaining brigade pulled out in October 1970, as did the 199th Light Infantry Brigade. The 4th Infantry Division departed for Fort Carson in December. In the same month the 25th Infantry Division returned to Hawaii, leaving one brigade behind for a few months.

The 173d Airborne Brigade had been in Vietnam before all of those units. It would remain after they were gone.

Then came 173d's turn. The Department of the Army ordered General MacFarlane to deactivate one of the 173d's four infantry battalions. Considering the tactical situation and expecting further deactivations, he picked 1st Battalion, 503d Infantry. That gallant unit was inactivated on April 27. Troopers with a long time remaining in Vietnam were transferred to the other three airborne infantry battalions. The 'short-timers' were shipped home. The battalion's colors were rolled up, cased in canvas, and shipped to the archives.

The brigade soldiered on into the summer.

Local RF/PF and regular ARVN units took on more of the security missions while most of the 173d reduced its field role.

Then word came from Washington to begin phasing the entire 173d out of Vietnam by the end of August. Orders were issued transferring it to Fort

NIGHT AMBUSH:
A Sky Trooper
of 3/503 waits
to surprise a
VC unit. By the
end of the
Vietnam War
the best units
had progressed
a long way
from the
attitude that
''night belongs
to Charlie.''

Campbell, Kentucky. Now the tough part began. The unit had to be withdrawn without jeopardizing the safety of the men. The 173d had to withdraw in good order in the face of a military threat. On a larger scale, it was similar to situations in cowboy novels, somewhat like the dirt farmer who has bumped into a nest of cattle rustlers in a saloon and tries to back through the swinging doors before they start shooting. In the event the withdrawal went calmly. The last flight of the 173d Airborne Brigade

(Separate) left Vietnam on August 25, 1971. That was six years, three months, and 20 days after the first C-130 touched down at Bien Hoa on May 5, 1965.

On December 17, 1971, the Army headquarters in Washington ordered the 173d Airborne Brigade deactivated. The order was carried out on January 14, 1972. On that day, the 173d Airborne Brigade (Separate) ended its active service.

The 173d was the only separate airborne brigade the US Army ever had. It never failed its country, and its Sky Soldiers never failed their leaders. They started with no history, a clean slate. In the brigade's eight years of existence and six-plus years of combat, they wrote a proud history of gallant service. The service of the thousands of men who were called Sky Soldiers set a standard of excellence for future generations of soldiers.

THE ENEMY: A captured VC combat engineer shows how under cover of darkness he would approach an American camp perimeter. Wearing few clothes to avoid the rustle of material, he carries an AK-47 assault rifle and a satchel pack containing explosive demolition charges. Often, the VC threw these into the perimeter wire to blast a pathway for the attacking force.

In Memoriam

A President Remembers

THE FOLLOWING address was given by President Ronald Reagan, at the May 1985 reunion of the 173d Airborne Brigade:

"I count it a real honor to speak this evening to the 'Sky Soldiers' — the veterans of the 173d Air borne Brigade. It is not often units in military history can claim the record of valor and devotion to duty that is yours — in less than a decade of existence, you received 12 Medals of Honor, 10 of them posthumous, and over 6,000 Purple Hearts. And — sadly but gallantly — there are today 1,533 names of your comrades carved in stone on the Vietnam Veterans Memorial.

"Those at least, are the statistics, but you know better than most that the cold statistics cannot tell the real story — maybe I should say 'the legend' — of the 173d. I think here of those early years in Vietnam; the first Army helicopter assault, the first joint-Allied operation, the only combat parachute assault, and of course the battle at Dak To — the calm and resolve of General Schweiter, the heroism of men like Chaplain Watters. What a record! As the years move back and history provides perspective, I can assure you that the deeds and dedication of 'The Herd' will be remembered as among the most illustrious in American military history. I could go on. But you know when I have been asked as President to talk at some occasion about the valor of our country's Armed Forces, I have often thought how right Lincoln was in the example he set at Gettysburg. When brave men have fought and died, there is little any president or person can add to the quiet testimony of their sacrifice.

"So tonight, I will do only what I can do as President: tell you that what you did in Vietnam lives

President Ronald Reagan

In Memoriam

AFTER THE BATTLE: Known as the Death Watch photo, this is the scene that brings back the agony of Vietnam for veterans of the 173d Brigade. Squad leader Sgt. Daniel E. Spencer (right) stares down at his fallen comrade while SP4 Rudiger Richter watches for a medevac helicopter through the lingering smoke of the firefight. It is August 1966 and the dead man was one of the first troopers of 4/503 to be killed in action.

on; that our commitment was a noble cause, that your deeds will always be remembered by free men and women — that someday, when freedom returns again to Southeast Asia, the people of those nations will honor you as surely as your countrymen honor you tonight.

"I wish you well on your reunion; I compliment those who have worked so hard on this project and all of

you for helping keep alive the great tradition of the Sky Soldiers of the 173d Airborne Brigade. And finally, I want to do what the American people would do if they had the chance to know your story and speak to you today. I want to thank each of you — for your valor, patriotism, and service to the cause of freedom, and for remembering your fallen and missing comrades. God bless you all."

AK-47	— Soviet 7.62mm automatic assault rifle (Kalashnikov).
APC	— Armored personnel carrier, usually M-113.
ARVN	— Army of the Republic of Vietnam.
Battery	— Artillery unit equivalent to infantry company.
Bde	— Brigade.
Bn	— Battalion.
Bunker	— Fighting position with overhead cover.
C & C ship	— Command and control helicopter.
CG	— Commanding general.
Charlie	— Nickname for the Viet Cong.
Claymore	— US command detonated antipersonnel mine used in perimeter defense and ambush. Throws pellets in a fan-shaped blast.
Co	— Company.
CO	— Commanding officer.
Cobra	— Attack helicopter AH-1G.
Cordon & search	— Operation in which an area is first sealed by a military force and then searched.
COSVN	— Central Office for South Vietnam (Communist Hq).
CP	— Command post.
CTZ	— Corps Tactical Zone (Vietnamese Army areas).
DEROS	— Rotation date—Date Eligible to Return from Overseas—the date a soldier was due to leave Vietnam.
Districts	— Level of South Vietnamese government structure subordinate to province. Comparable to US county.
Dustoff	— Helicopter extraction, usually medical.
FAC	— Forward Air Controller; USAF pilot attached to ground unit to control air strikes.
FFV	— Field Force, Vietnam (US Hq at corps level).
FO	— Forward observer—operates in

combat areas adjusting ground and naval fire, and air bombardment.

SKY SOLDIERS

Glossary

FSB — Fire Support Base, a defended perimeter containing supporting artillery and mortar units.

Gunship — Armed helicopter.

Hq — Headquarters.

Huey — UH-1 utility helicopter.

LAW — M72 Light Antitank Weapon (66mm) with shaped charge.

LRP — Long range patrol.

LZ — Landing zone.

MACV — Military Assistance Command, Vietnam.

NVA — North Vietnamese Army.

PF — Popular Forces. Military forces recruited and employed within a district.

POW — Prisoner of war.

Province — Political subdivision of Vietnam comparable to a state in the US.

RF — Regional forces. Military forces recruited and employed within a province; organized as companies.

RPG — Rocket propelled grenade.

RTO — Radio-telephone operator.

RVN — Republic of Vietnam.

S-1 — Personnel staff officer at Battalion and Brigade.

S-2 — Intelligence staff officer at those levels.

S-3 — Operations & training staff officer at those levels.

S-4 — Logistics officer at those levels.

S-5 — Civil affairs officer at those levels.

Sapper — NVA or VC demolitions expert.

SOP — Standing Operating Procedure.

TAOR — Tactical Area of Responsibility.

Task Force — Temporary grouping of units under one commander, for a specific operation or mission.

TOC — Tactical operations center.

VC — Viet Cong.

About the Author

F.Clifton Berry, Jr.

F.Clifton Berry, Jr., was a paratrooper and airborne infantry officer in the 82d Airborne Division. He saw Vietnam combat as operations officer of the 196th Light Infantry Brigade.

In an army career, he commanded airborne and infantry units from squad through battalion level in the US and Far East.

Following active service, since 1975 he has been an editor and writer on military and aerospace topics. He was co-editor of Armed Forces Journal, editor in chief of Air Force Magazine, and chief US editor of the Interavia publishing group. He is a master parachutist and active pilot, with land and seaplane ratings.

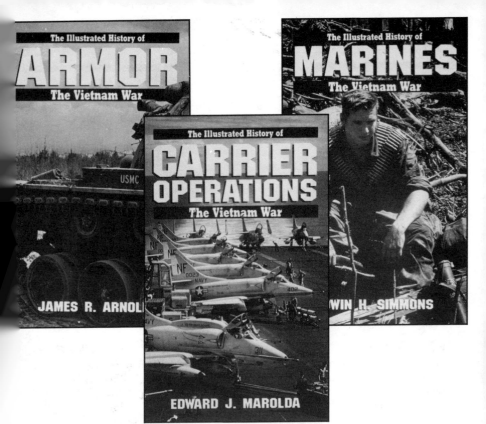

THE ILLUSTRATED HISTORY OF THE VIETNAM WAR

Bantam's Illustrated History of the Vietnam War is a unique and new series of books exploring in depth the war that seared America to the core: A war that cost 58,022 American lives, that saw great heroism and resourcefulness mixed with terrible destruction and tragedy.

The Illustrated History of the Vietnam War examines exactly what happened: every significant aspect—the physical details, the operations and the strategies behind them—is analyzed in short, crisply written original books by established historians and journalists.

Some books are devoted to key battles and campaigns, others unfold the stories of elite groups and fighting units, while others focus on the role of specific weapons and tactics.

Each volume is totally original and is richly illustrated with photographs, line drawings, and maps.